SALAMANCA

THE DESIGN
OF EXECUTIVE
PROTECTION
SYSTEMS

THE DESIGN
OF EXECUTIVE
PROTECTION
SYSTEMS

By

JOE B. FLYNN, M.S.

Special Agent
Staff Manager of Criminal Investigations
United States Air Force Office of Special Investigations

CHARLES   C   THOMAS   •   PUBLISHER
Springfield • Illinois • U.S.A.

Published and Distributed Throughout the World by

CHARLES C THOMAS ● PUBLISHER

Bannerstone House

301-327 East Lawrence Avenue, Springfield, Illinois, U.S.A.

© *1979, by* CHARLES C THOMAS ● PUBLISHER

ISBN 0-398-03894-5

Library of Congress Catalog Card Number: 78-26316

With THOMAS BOOKS *careful attention is given to all details of
manufacturing and design. It is the Publisher's desire to present books that
are satisfactory as to their physical qualities and artistic possibilities and
appropriate for their particular use.* THOMAS BOOKS *will be true to those
laws of quality that assure a good name and good will.*

Printed in the United States of America
V-R-1

Library of Congress Cataloging in Publication Data

Flynn, Joe B
    The design of executive protection systems

    Bibliography: p. 85
    Includes index.
    1. Corporations--Security measures.
2. Industry--Security measures. I. Title.
HV8290.F58   658.4'7   78-26316
ISBN 0-398-03894-5

PREFACE

THE intent of this effort is to provide security managers with a tool with which they might succeed in defining, shaping, and implementing a viable protective service for their individual corporations. To even the most casual observer of world news, the threat of violence appears to be growing logarithmically while successful innovations in personnel protection advance at only a linear rate.

It is hoped that the guidance and suggestions offered within these pages will measurably assist the security response to keep pace with the demands imposed by the threat. The book is designed to serve as advisor to individual efforts. It takes a systematic approach, leading the manager-designer from the initial idea through the design and implementation stages of an executive protection system.

CONTENTS

THE DESIGN
OF EXECUTIVE
PROTECTION
SYSTEMS

CHAPTER 1

Introduction

THERE exists within our society a propensity for violence that grows more alarming with each passing year. A combination of the availability of weapons, the sociological aggrandizement of immediate actions, and constitutionally guaranteed individual freedoms has created conditions alimentative of this violence. Elitist groups and disturbed individuals, viewing terrorism as legitimate political means, have perpetrated acts so shocking to the majority as to generate an undercurrent of fear throughout the nation. This fear has proven disruptive to the conventional political process and seriously affects both corporate and private enterprise.

Claud Fly, a 1970 kidnap victim, stated in his testimony before Congress (*Terrorism*, Part 3, pp. 3963-78, 1974) concerning this threat:

> Because the psychological and social effects of kidnapping are so devastating, there is justification for using even the most drastic means to prevent their occurrence and lessen the danger of threat of such antisocial behavior. An understanding of the basic causes of violent, antisocial action on the part of individuals and groups is a necessary adjunct to developing preventative and protective measures.

Acts of terrorism, both organizationally and individually accomplished, are so replete as to have become practically a news staple. The victims of terrorism are found among varying occupational and professional groups, political hopefuls, industrial leaders, and diplomatic corps alike.

Robert Kennedy, speaking on June 2, 1968, said "Men

3

are not made for safe havens." Four days later, in a San Francisco hotel, his life was ended by an assassin. President John F. Kennedy, on November 22, 1963, had met a similar fate while motoring down a Dallas street. The Reverend Martin Luther King, Jr. found no safe haven on April 4, 1968, as he stood talking with friends on his Memphis hotel balcony.

Victor Samuelson, manager of a Campana, Argentina Esso oil refinery, was kidnapped from his breakfast table on December 6, 1973. His abductors, members of the People's Revolutionary Army (ERP), released him following the payment of $14,200,000 by Esso.

On September 4, 1969, a Brazilian urban guerrilla organization known as Movimiento Revolucionario-8 (MR-8) kidnapped the U.S. Ambassador to Brazil, C. Burk Elbrick, while enroute from his residence to the embassy. MR-8 demanded the release of fifteen political prisoners and publication of the MR-8 manifesto throughout the Brazilian media within forty-eight hours or Elbrick was to be executed. Under pressure from the United States, the Brazilian government complied with these demands, flying the prisoners to Mexico City, and Elbrick was released in Rio de Janeiro, Brazil.

These are but isolated instances, illustrative of the necessity for comprehensive systems of protection for specific occupational groups. Perhaps Kennedy was correct that men are not meant for safe havens, but surely they are deserving of some modicum of security while performing their duties. The number of kidnappings, bombings, hijackings, and murders has assumed phenomenal proportions in recent years. Novelist Albert Camus was prophetic in describing the twentieth century as the century of fear.

Seemingly, the major threat is generated by the small elite groups and the individual assassin. Historically, large-scale endeavors by radical American groups have ended in failure. In August of 1969, the Black Liberation Front (BLF) engaged in such action in Pittsburgh, Pennsylvania. For a period of three days, the northern Three Rivers section of that city was the scene of a pitched battle between BLF-inspired rioters and Pennsylvania National Guard troops combined with city police. At the conclusion of this affray, more than seventy-five rioters were injured, many of whom were women and children, and thousands of dollars of property damage occurred. The injuries to law enforcement personnel were minimal.

Large-scale actions such as those previously described are invariably met by overpowering forces and are doomed to failure from the beginning. Through the careful selection of an individual target, a particular industrialist for example, terrorists enhance their potential of success, realizing that this type of target seldom results in massive military retaliation on the part of the government. Properly executed, these operations produce even greater results than do large-scale strikes. Also, they do not alienate people, turning them against the movement, as do incidents involving the destruction of private property.

The psychological and social effects referred to by Fly are not entirely accidental by-products of terrorism but are carefully planned and integral parts of it. Assassination and kidnapping are but the tools used to produce maximum impact, accomplished with assurance that the activity will receive media attention. This attention is guaranteed if the activity is accompanied by mutilation of the victim. This also serves to heighten the fear generated (Momboisse, 1970).

Fly spoke of the need for development of preventative and protective measures; it is this need to which this book is addressed. In establishing a system of protective services, issues arise involving ethical, moral, philosophical, and of necessity, financial significance.

The goal of this effort is to deal with these issues and to produce a guide to be utilized in the initial establishment of personnel security programs. The final product is not intended to be a "cookbook" from which one might take an ounce of policy, a cup of intelligence, and a teaspoon of protective hardware, mix it well, and spread it over the organization, thereby assuring adequate protection to those within. In short, this book is designed to be an aid, not a panacea, for those about to implement an executive protection service.

This is by no means a definitive work, expounding on every aspect and technological innovation of physical and personnel protection. It is designed as a stimulus for creative activity on the part of the security manager-designer and should assist in channeling his individual energies in directions productive of a realistic and personalized system.

It is assumed that the reader will possess at least a minimal degree of expertise within the field of security, so ultraelaborate detail describing the more common items of hardware is deliberately omitted. It is presumed that a generalized discussion of these items will serve as a trigger mechanism, refreshing previously accumulated knowledge of the subject. Specific areas with which the reader is unfamiliar should serve as flags of warning, encouraging additional research into those particular aspects of security. The reader will find the bibliography of great assistance in this search.

The objectives of this book are twofold: (1) to explore the three environments of the executive: professional, residential, and transitory; and (2) to examine corporate policy concerning indoctrination of corporate personnel, direction and scope of the program, and the training required.

Significance

This book is intended for use by the private, as opposed to the governmental, sector. The question might well be posed, "Of what significance is such an effort, considering the numbers of federal, state, and local law enforcement and intelligence agencies now in existence?" This question is best answered by defining those who are most threatened by terrorism and assault.

Those persons most threatened by terrorists or individual assault can be divided into four status groups: imposed, traditional, ideological, and representative. Of these four categories, the status group that can least avail itself of the vast resources of the government is that of the representative status. It is this group, located primarily within the private sector, that will derive the greatest benefit from this guide.

To determine the membership of an individual within a specific status group, one must examine the particular circumstances and situation in which that individual is functioning. Essentially the division is accomplished as follows.

IMPOSED STATUS: Those individuals whose lives are endangered through the assumption of an active role within the criminal justice system are, for example, witnesses, prosecutors, investigators, and judges.

TRADITIONAL STATUS: Those persons whose lives are placed in jeopardy with the assumption of an official position are for example, the President and Vice President of the United States, diplomats, and, of late, officially recognized candidates for these positions. This category or status is separate from the imposed status target because of the continuous existence of the threat. The witness, prosecutor, investigator, and judge are targets only when their responsibility imposes a particular action on them. They are normally no longer targets following the passage of this responsibility, that is, the end of a trial. Targets of traditional status remain targets throughout the tenure of their official positions, and often for a period following such tenure, regardless of their current activity or inactivity.

IDEOLOGICAL STATUS: Individuals within this particular status group have, because of personal convictions, "placed themselves in harms' way." Within this group are found the civil rights activists, gay rights leaders, spokesmen of the Ku Klux Klan, and so forth. It might be said of this particular status that their vulnerability is dependent upon their individual avocation rather than upon their vocation.

REPRESENTATIVE STATUS: These individuals occupy a position within a socioeconomic structure that lends impact to their activities. They are the directors of corporations and the possessors of wealth, individuals whose image is that of being representative of their social strata. It is within this group that one finds the Gettys, the Hursts, the Rockefellers, and the decision makers of U.S. Steel, Esso, Tenneco, and other major industries.

It can be said that the protection of individuals within these four groups has been delegated, either formally or informally, to specific agencies or entities. Protection of the imposed and traditional status targets has been entrusted to agencies at the governmental level, federal or state. Such agencies include the Secret Service, U.S. Marshals, the Federal Bureau of Investigation, Justice Department, and state police, to name but a few.

Protection of the ideological status target has evolved into a shared task, generally involving local police, occasionally state police, and, infrequently, federal agencies. The protection is extended over the period of time the individual is involved in a specific activity, such as a rally, and only expands to private life during a period that there exists a known threat against the person.

Representative status targets are seldom recipients of local, state, or federal protective services except as a by-product of their immediate involvement with one or more of the other status groups. Protection of this category has become the responsibility of private efforts and, unlike the other three, is funded by the individual or by the industry with which he is predominately affiliated.

This is not meant to imply that a specific individual can occupy only one status at one time. Quite the contrary, an individual will often hold a dual status, for example, the civil rights activist who is called to testify against someone or some group accused of violating the rights of another. In this case the target is holding a dual status, that of imposed and ideological groupings.

As indicated in the introductory section of this chapter, terrorism is an increasing threat at all levels. Since 1968, eighty-two diplomats and other United States officials have been kidnapped or otherwise subjected to terrorists attacks, the result being thirty-three kidnappings, eighteen murders, and thirty-one wounded (Fromkin, 1975). While agencies exist at local, state, and federal levels whose stated and implied purpose is to provide protection to the citizens of their respective jurisdictions, one must understand that the response by these agencies is normally reactive in nature, that is, after the fact. Protection, especially for the representative status group, prior to the occurrence of an antisocial act is dependent upon the resources of the private sector.

Through utilization of this guide, as well as other pertinent sources, it might become possible to limit the degree of susceptibility to such acts. This book is significant in that it attempts to establish preventive rather than prosecutorial protection. It is designed to save lives rather than to apprehend the assassin of an executive.

Specific terms used in this guide might not be imme-

diately understood by the reader. To avoid any confusion
or misunderstanding caused by this, a list of definitions
follows.

Definitions

CLANDESTINE: Activity conducted in such a way as to insure secrecy or concealment. Differs from covert in that
the emphasis is on concealment of the activity as well as
concealment of the actor.

COLLECTION: The obtaining of information in any
manner, to include direct observation, liaison with official agencies, or solicitation from any official, unoffi-
cial, or public source.

COVERT: Activity conducted in such a way as to conceal
identity or permit plausible denial by the sponsor.
Differs from clandestine in that emphasis is on concealment of the activity or operation.

DISSIDENCE: Activities that actively encourage violation of
the law, disobedience of lawful order, or disruption of
corporate activities.

ESPIONAGE: Overt, covert, or clandestine activity designed
to obtain information relating to an executive or organization with intent or reason to believe that it will be
used to the injury of the executive or corporation, or to
the advantage of an outside individual or organization.

GOVERNMENTAL SECTOR: That societal structure consisting
of public servants, both elected and appointed, whose
salaries are paid from collected taxes and whose agencies
are budgeted through taxation.

HARDWARE: A term encompassing any electrical, electronic, or mechanical device whose major purpose is the
enhancement of security, either physical or personnel, of
the recipient organization of the protective service.

• HIGH PROFILE: A term used to describe the highest category of protection available. A very visible form of pro-

tection incorporating bodyguards, armored transportation, and fortified lodgings.

• LOW PROFILE: Security at the opposite end of the spectrum from high profile. This incorporates little security hardware and is primarily dependent upon instruction to individuals concerning the avoidance of risk and proper security habits.

MASTER KEY: A key controlling a number of locks, each of which is also controlled by its own independent key. A mastered system refers to a series of locking devices designed so that each has a separate key but can be opened by one master key.

OVERT: Any activity undertaken without regard to concealment of either the activity or its sponsor.

•PERSONNEL SECURITY INVESTIGATION: An inquiry into the activities of an individual, designed to develop pertinent information with respect to the trustworthiness of that individual, suitability for a position of trust, loyalty, character, emotional stability, and reliability.

PRIVATE SECTOR: That societal structure composed of individually or jointly owned and controlled enterprises engaged in supplying a service or product in return for monetary profit and not funded through tax dollars.

• PROFESSIONAL ENVIRONMENT: That environment in which the executive normally performs his corporate duties and discharges his professional responsibilities. Normally it is considered to be within the structure commonly referred to as the plant or office. This can vary in some isolated instances, depending upon the duties of a specific executive; for example, the environment of a public relations executive would overlap with the transitory environment in that he would perform his official duties in numerous locations.

• RESIDENTIAL ENVIRONMENT: That environment in which the executive and his family live, their home or apartment. This would include the grounds, if any, surrounding the residence. Places of temporary lodging, that is, a hotel or motel room, would not be considered as residential but as transitory in nature.

RISK: The variation in the possible outcomes that exists in nature in a given situation. When risk is small, one's ability to predict the future is high; when the risk is great, one's ability to predict the future is low.

SABOTAGE: An act with the intent to injure, interfere with, obstruct, or impair the function of the corporation by willfully injuring or destroying, or attempting to destroy or injure, any corporate property, premises, or utility, to include human and natural resources.

• SECURITY: Any measure taken by, or in behalf of, a corporation element that affords protection against acts designed to, or which might, impair its effectiveness.

SUBVERSION: Actions designed to undermine the loyalty, morale, or discipline of corporate security personnel or other corporate employees.

SURVEILLANCE: The observation or monitoring of persons, places, or things by visual, aural, photographic, electronic, or other physical means that are intended for the purpose of obtaining information.

TARGET: An entity (organization, group, physical structure, or individual) against which antisocial actions are directed or intelligence efforts are expended.

• TRANSITORY ENVIRONMENT: That environment in which an executive finds himself when traveling from his home to his place of business or vice versa. This environment also would include periods when the executive is traveling from one place of business to another.

CHAPTER 2

The Issue

THERE seem to exist certain assumptions on the parts of many individuals, particularly within the United States, that terrorist activities most often occur in Europe or the Middle East and therefore are not of great concern to the American citizen. This concept generates a false sense of security. In reality, United States citizens have been the victims in one-third of all terrorists attacks throughout the world since 1968 (Tannenbaum, 1977).

Yet another myth is the image of terrorists, held by perhaps the majority of uninformed people. They see the terrorist as being poor, hungry idealists. Laqueur (1976) pointed out that as often as not, modern terrorism is "big business." The Palestinian Liberation Organization (PLO), for example, has an annual income in excess of $200 million. Many other major terrorist organizations have also amassed many millions of dollars.

The manager of a corporate security system must assume that the executives of his organization are indeed in danger. He must realize that terrorist groups, possessing the wealth that many of them do, can avail themselves of the most modern weapons and technology, thereby amplifying the potential threat. Terrorism has become a distinctive disorder of modern society whereby groups too small to impose their will by force have resorted to intimidation and blackmail to realize their objectives.

Though governmental entities are the ultimate target in most cases, it is the individual, most often from the representative status group, who becomes the victim of terrorist attack. Lineberry (1977, p. 5) recalled a passage from the *London Economist* that accurately describes this condition:

> If you are filled with rage because the twentieth century is as imperfect as the others, or because the injustice that hurts you most has not been removed from the world, or just because you cannot get other people to agree with you, you are entitled to grab the first person you see on the street and hold him at gunpoint in a cellar until the government buys you off.

When terrorists strike out at society, they are taking a calculated risk, but one far smaller than most would imagine. The Rand Corporation recently reported that, based upon a study of international terrorist acts since 1968, there was an 80 percent chance that a terrorist-kidnapper would escape death or capture; a 50 percent chance that at least a portion of the demands would be realized; and a 100 percent chance that all the publicity sought would be received. This study revealed that of the 267 international terrorists apprehended since 1970, less than one-half were still in jail as of September, 1975. The average prison sentence was but eighteen months (Fearey, 1976).

When faced with the task of designing a viable system of executive protection, the security manager must deal with two pressing questions: From what source will the threat originate, and what countermeasures are available to him? The first question might be answered in very general terms by stating that the threat will come from either a terrorist-type organization or an individual assailant. If one protects himself from the former, he will automatically generate a high degree of security with respect to the latter.

This is of course a very generalized answer and does not attempt to identify specifically those organizations or individuals. Identification is a task which will become, for the security manager, a dynamic and ongoing concern. It is dependent upon the geographic location of the target and the current sociopolitical environment.

The second portion of the question, that of the available countermeasures, is in itself a considerable assignment. To begin with, there is, on the part of those agencies employing systems of executive protection, a general reluctance to discuss this practice. This reluctance, although posing difficulties for the would-be designer, is understandable. It reflects a genuine concern on the part of security directors based on a widespread and well-founded conviction that to divulge operational information concerning a particular system is automatically to weaken that system.

It is only with great hesitancy that the manager of such a program will enter into a broad discussion of protective theories with an outsider, fearing that this discussion will allow the other party to learn, through inference, the operation of his own specific system. This is particularly true if the interviewed perceives the interviewer as possessing a background in security.

While this reluctance does pose problems, they are not insurmountable. Information concerning security is available to the researcher; seldom does one encounter a library devoid of books dealing with the subjects of terrorism, risk management, residential security, and other related topics. The difficulty lies in the accumulation, analysis, interpretation, editing, and reproduction of the available material, thereby generating a comprehensive treatment isomorphic to reality.

Yet another problem encountered by the corporation embarking for the first time into the design of an executive or plant security program is that of integrity. Assume that the corporate executives, realizing their own limitations in the area of security design, bring in an outside source of expertise. The final product will be compromised in its genesis. It will lack integrity in that an outsider will possess an intimate knowledge of the overall system. Should the outside expert turn to assistants for advice or corroboration during the initial design, the final system will suffer even greater compromise.

The suggested system, when submitted to the corporation, will have to be accepted blindly, for the corporation has no expertise and therefore no way adequately to assess the quality. Had the necessary skill existed in the beginning, there would have been no need to enlist the aid of an outsider.

The major danger lies not in the potential for compromise, but in the potential of implementing a less than adequate system. It can be assumed that the outside expert might be honest, but if he is incompetent and this goes undetected, there will result a false sense of security within the implementing corporation. This false sense of security, resulting from placing confidence in a weak system, is in many ways more dangerous than having no system at all. Lulled into feeling that they are amply protected, executives will begin to assume risks that they otherwise would guard against.

The initial question concerning the origin of the threat should motivate the security manager to research the problem of terrorism. While he need not become an expert in the field of history nor of motivation, he does require an understanding of the tactics and strategy of the historical masters of the art.

It is equally important that the security manager does not allow himself to stereotype the leaders of current movements, categorizing them as being societal dropouts and losers. A recent examination of terrorism within the United States pointed out that those attracted to terrorism seldom actually belong to the class for which they profess to be fighting (Alexander, 1976). A brief examination of the leadership of two major terrorist organizations of the past twenty years tends to support this contention.

The Leadership

The Weathermen faction of the Students for Democratic Society (SDS) and the Symbionese Liberation Army (SLA) both professed to represent a utopian society requiring one to murder and bomb to realize attainment. These two groups were, by and large, composed of literate and articulate young people claiming to have highly developed philosophic reasons for their actions, although the SLA never actually detailed the purposes of its demanded revolution.

The Weathermen were hampered by the presence of many leaders and few followers, a combination guaranteeing ultimate failure in almost any venture. Seeking to gain recruits, they planned a series of sensational daylight escapades to organize the disenfranchised and alienated street gangs of the major cities. The blatant acts of violence were intended to so impress the members of these gangs that they would join the fight against the establishment. Although this failed to take place, the Weathermen never forsook their avowed violence. John Jacobs, one of the leaders, even made the public statement, "We're against everything that's good and decent." (Adelson, 1972, p. 242). Bernardine Dohrn, speaking of Charles Manson and his followers, said "Dig it! First they killed the pigs, then they even shoved a fork in the victim's stomach! Wild!" (Adelson, 1972, p. 247).

The birth of the SLA was unique. Unlike the Weathermen, they were not a splinter group; their organization began with a group of educated, idealistic would-be revolutionists who began visiting, ostensibly to teach, the semiliterate convicts incarcerated in the San Francisco Bay area prisons.

Once embarked on this mission, these students found the nucleus of the perfect revolutionary organization in a few inmates. These convicts were totally alienated and dehumanized by the prison system (Alexander, 1976). They were well versed in violence and unfettered by moral convictions. Once out of their cells, these two factions united to form this terrorist army.

The SLA soldiers were a strange mixture for a revolutionary army. Angel de Angelis Atwood was a former cheerleader from New Jersey whose father was a trade union official. Another member, Nancy Ling Perry, had worked for the 1964 Goldwater campaign. Perry had a degree in English but chose to operate a fruit stand rather than enter what she saw as the bourgeois career ladder.

Other teacher-soldiers included the daughter of a California pharmacist, Patricia Saltysik, and the daughter of a Lutheran minister, Camilla Hall. Hall was a one-time social worker with a degree from the University of Minnesota. Russell Little was the exception to the group; he had dropped out of the University of Florida and traveled to California seeking adventure.

The SLA members who had come from the prisons included the eventual leader, Donald DeFreeze. He came out of Soledad prison with a long history of petty offenses and mental illness. His close friend, Joe Reniro, was a Vietnam veteran with expertise in weaponry.

The first leap into the public eye by the SLA came with the murder of Marcus Foster, the black school superintendent of Oakland. Foster was killed with cyanide bullets following his announcement that he intended to issue student identification cards at local schools in an effort to control entry onto campus. This would have hampered SLA recruitment efforts so Foster was murdered.

The second and by far the best-publicized activity was that of the kidnapping and conversion of Patricia Hurst. The SLA story ended in May, 1974 when they were surrounded by approximately 150 Los Angeles policemen and 100 FBI agents. The ensuing gunfight killed 6 members of the SLA.

The Threat

Organizations operating today continue to draw inspiration and justification from the major revolutionaries of history. There exists no end of materials expounding the endeavors of Mao Tse-tung, Che Guevara, and Carlos Marighella and describing in detail the activities of such organizations as the Irish Republican Army (IRA), the Black Panthers, the Black September Movement, and the SLA.

Marighella in particular has written of guerrilla tactics with such style and intensity that his writings have become gospel for many would-be urban guerrillas today. His views on terrorist activities and the detailed manner of his writing have given current groups a blueprint for terrorism.

Modern terrorists, like their historical forerunners, view violence as a purifying force, freeing one from inferiority complexes and from the despair of inactivity. In the minds of political radical leaders, the elitists, there exists a certain mystique of action. To them violence is a means to restore self-respect.

"When in doubt burn. Fire is the revolutionary's god." This statement was made by Jerry Rubin, leader of the American Yippies (Mallin, 1971, p. 76). A captured SLA document also reflects this action philosophy (Mallin, 1971, p. 132):

> It is the responsibility of the Armament Unit to build facilities for the making of machine guns, reloading equipment, cyanide bombs and bullets, acquiring or building antitank weapons, flame throwers and explosives.

The American "movements" have historically had little, if any, program and so tended toward opportunism. It has been their belief that a program would develop out of action. It was this type of concept Bertrand Russell referred to as "thinking with the blood."

There are those for whom action is important in itself, a kind of existential reaction to the overly technological society of the United States. These groups feel a sense of betrayal by so-called liberals whose theories and aspirations seemingly end in futility. Change is too slow in coming so they resort to action.

Eldrige Cleaver made this comment when he first witnessed members of the Black Panther Party for Self Defense (Cleaver, 1968, p. 21):

> I . . . saw the most beautiful sight I had ever seen: four black men wearing black berets, powder-blue shirts, black leather jackets, black trousers . . . and each with a gun.

Mark Rudd, leader of the Weathermen faction of the SDS, is quoted as follows (Adelson, 1972, p. 213):

> We do have a vision of the way things could be: How the tremendous resources of our economy could be used to eliminate want . . . how men could be free to keep what they produce, to enjoy peaceful lives, to create . . . We will have to destroy at times, even violently, in order to end your (capitalist system).

The Techniques

Work disruptions through subversion and dissidence, destruction of corporate products accompanied by sabotage, and other techniques are available to terrorist organizations. Despite the spectrum of tactics upon which they could draw, terrorists have traditionally relied heavily upon three activities: kidnapping, bombing, and assassination.

Kidnapping is a particularly useful device since it focuses attention on a particular target, usually symbolic of a group or organization. The victim of kidnapping can be manipulated for propaganda purposes and might also serve as a source of additional revenue for the movement. Revenue is no small consideration on the part of terrorists. Bunge and Born Company, a giant conglomerate in Argentina, paid $60 million for the ransom and release of two kidnapped executives (Adelson, 1972).

Even the release of a kidnapped victim can serve propaganda purposes, demonstrating that the terrorists have the ability to choose their victims at will. Oppenheimer (1969, p. 34) states:

> (Terrorism) can be discriminatory in its victims or indiscriminate in its violence . . . indiscriminate terrorism tends to be more disruptive; discriminate terrorism more politically symbolic.

Marighella (1971, pp. 62-63) saw as the responsibility of the urban guerrilla:

> (To) baffle, discredit and harass the military and other forces of repression, and to destroy or loot goods belonging to North Americans, the heads of foreign firms, or the Brazilian upper class.

He also saw logic in kidnapping and set forth a checklist by which the potential kidnapper might enhance his expectation of success. Marighella (1971, p. 74) urged the guerrilla to use the following methods:

1. Careful inquiry and analysis of information
2. Observation
3. Reconnaissance
4. Study and timing of routes
5. Mapping
6. Transportation
7. Selection of personnel
8. Selection of firing ability and capacity
9. Simulation of action
10. Execution of action
11. Cover for those who execute action
12. Withdrawal

13. Removal of wounded
14. Destruction of clues

He was so explicit in his writings that he has become a source for both the terrorist and the security manager. Marighella (1971, p. 76) formulated a listing of urban actions, linking them with their targets, and urged the practitioner to incorporate them as part of an overall strategy and not isolated instances. These actions included the following:

1. Attacks or raids upon banks and radio stations
2. Burglaries of offices and government buildings
3. Ambush of police, businessmen, and army personnel
4. Strikes and other work disruptions at factories and schools
5. Theft of arms and explosives from armories, police stations, and factories
6. Execution of spies and police informants
7. Kidnapping of police, political figures, and businessmen
8. Sabotage and arson directed against factories, banks, transportation, and communications facilities

It is this attention to detail that has made Marighella so very important to security managers.

Additional materials are available that point out the importance of executive training in regard to kidnapping. Sir Geoffery Jackson, British Ambassador to Uruguay, was kidnapped in January, 1971. He has since published a book concerning this experience and the importance of proper training (Jackson, 1974).

Realizing the potential danger of kidnapping, Jackson established a series of ruses to attempt to delay kidnap efforts and distract the attention of the attackers, as well as theories of possible escape attempts. When his kidnapping occurred, Jackson feigned a heart attack and felt that he would have been able to escape as a result, had there been suitable cover nearby where he could have hidden.

Assassination, the second and perhaps most powerful weapon in the terrorist arsenal, has been treated by all major revolutionary writers. Concerning this tactic, Marighella stated (1971, p. 87):

> We should use the death penalty for such people as American spies, agents of the dictatorship . . . fascists in the government who have committed crimes against the patriots or tried to capture them. . . . Such executions must be carried out in secret, with the smallest number of guerrillas involved. Quite often a single sniper, patient and unknown. . . .

When thinking in terms of a single assassin, particularly with respect to executive protection, one is well advised to consider the description offered by Forsyth (1971, p. 342) of the professional assassin:

> A professional . . . is therefore more calm and less likely to make elementary errors . . . he is not likely to have second thoughts at the last minute about who might get hurt in the explosion or whatever method, and being a professional he has calculated the risks to the last contingency. So his chances of success on schedule are surer than anyone else's.

Momboisse (1970) further described the terrorist use of assassination, calling the liquidation of "enemy" leadership a favorite device of the terrorist. He pointed out that assassinations are frequently planned in great detail, with the target studied carefully, his habits, routes of travel, times of passage of specific points, and precautionary measures noted. Once a pattern has been established, the time and place of the assassination has been determined. Escape routes are plotted, men deployed to prevent pursuit, and success estimated.

When Oppenheimer (1969) referred to indiscriminate terrorism as being the most disruptive, he might well have had in mind the third favorite technique of terrorism, the use of bombs. No form of terrorism is more disruptive nor instills greater fear than the use of explosives.

Essentially, explosives are substances capable of rapid conversion from solid or liquid form to a gaseous state with resultant heat and pressure. The resultant rate of expansion varies from substance to substance, allowing explosive materials to be classified as either high or low explosive (Svensson and Wendel, 1965).

Low explosives are generally considered to be those expanding at a rate of approximately 3,000 feet per second. High explosives, on the other hand, expand at rates in excess of 15,000 feet per second. Most current high explosives contain essentially a mixture of nitrocellulose with nitroglycerine or nitroglycol and ammonium nitrate (Walls, 1974).

Terrorists' choice of explosives to accomplish their goals can be explained in several ways. First, one need not even plant the explosive charge to realize disruptive results. A simple telephone threat will accomplish this end. Should one decide to carry out a planned bombing, programmed delay between the placement and the explosion will allow time for the terrorist to relocate himself miles from the scene. It is even possible for a terrorist to evaluate public reaction to a specific explosion prior to claiming credit for the act. In many cases, one group will attempt to claim the credit for the act of another.

Like kidnapping, bombing focuses attention on specific targets and insures maximum media coverage. With bombings, there are limitations imposed by the complexity of some explosive devices that result in their use only by those groups having as a member someone possessing at least some expertise.

While kidnapping, assassination, and bombing represent the three most predominant terrorist activities, there are at least nine categories of tactics common to the vast majority of terrorist acts (Private Security Advisory

Council to LEAA, 1976, pp. 3-4).

1. The use of violence as a method of systematic persuasion
2. The selection of targets and victims with maximum propaganda value
3. The use of unprovoked attacks
4. The selection of acts that gain maximum publicity with the minimum risk to the terrorist
5. The use of surprise to overcome countermeasures
6. The use of threats, harassment, and violence to create an atmosphere of fear
7. The use of propaganda to maximize the effects of violence and to achieve political or economical goals
8. The lack of recognition of civilians or women and children as noncombatants
9. The perpetration of terroristic acts by groups whose only loyalty is to each other

While current terrorist forces might draw inspiration from Marighella and Guevara, they can also realize instruction from more recent sources. William Powell authored a book, appropriately entitled *The Anarchist Cookbook* (1971, p. 61), in which he details the essentials of terrorist enterprize, the reader being given step-by-step instructions in such arts as explosive and weapons manufacturing and drawings of effective booby traps. Powell seeks to justify acts of terrorism by quoting Abraham Lincoln:

> This country, with its institutions, belongs to the people who inhabit it. Whenever they shall grow weary of the existing Government, they can exercise their constitutional right of amending it, or their revolutionary right to dismember or overthrow it.

Although not strong on philosphy or ideology, Powell does render a volume of "practical" advice on topics like knife attacks, listing the most vulnerable points of the human antomy, and how to rig booby traps and create homemade bombs, as well as tips on sabotage.

The Private Security Advisory Council Report (1976, p. 1) points out that ". . . the terrorist underground operates in hard-to-infiltrate small groups, rendering public law enforcement less capable of thwarting their activities." This makes it doubly important for the private sector to attempt to minimize the risk of such attacks by providing a before-the-fact program of individual protection.

CHAPTER 3

The Response

RECOGNITION of the existence and scope of terrorism is but a conditioning step. The major problem lies in the formulation of adequate countermeasures, the response to the problem. The individual security designer or director cannot be expected to solve the basic problem, that of the existence of terrorism; his responsibility is the creation of a shield against this threat.

The final solution to the overall issue, if it truly can be solved, must take place on a broad international level. Since there has been a demonstrated inability on the part of nations to jointly cope with terrorism, it is logical that unilateral steps must be taken.

Fearey (1975) suggested a number of means by which terrorism can be opposed. He cites more effective intelligence networks, enhanced physical security, the elimination of the profit motive, and attempts to eliminate the underlying causes of terrorism as the corrective needs.

We must begin to recognize terrorism for what it truly represents, global criminality. Once apprehended, terrorists must be punished to the full extent of the law, and nations must seek to establish extradition agreements between themselves in order to facilitate the return of terrorists to the country in which the act occurred where they can stand trial.

The most powerful weapon with which to counter terrorism is the employment of highly sophisticated intelligence networks. This means the utilization of the entire spectrum of clandestine means: wiretaps, bugs, spies, paid informants, all of those techniques so susceptible to attack by the civil-libertarian forces. In 1957, a British Privy

27

Council Committee on wiretapping reported its opinion that the freedom of the individual was quite valueless if that individual could be made the victim of the law-breaker. The proper use of technological aides only enhances the true freedom of the individual (Fromkin, 1975).

Still another response to terrorism lies in the reevaluation of emphasis placed upon their deeds by the media. This is not an advocation of censorship, it is a call to the responsible members of the news media to avoid acting in unwitting concert with the desires of the terrorist. Hickey (1976) suggests the following steps be taken by the media:

1. Refrain from presenting "how-to" coverage, showing in detail how specific acts are accomplished.
2. Downplay or omit the names of terrorist groups and thereby deny them the expected and coveted publicity while still giving viewers news of the crime itself.
3. Limit live coverage of crimes involving hostages since this can often endanger their lives by hampering or prematurely exposing rescue attempts.
4. Give proper emphasis to the inhuman aspects of terrorism and avoid lending the impression that it is exciting and somehow romantic.
5. Refrain from interviewing terrorist leaders on television and thereby lending them the air of respectability.

Many measures designed to improve security have been instituted, including the improvements in airport security, greater awareness on the part of corporate security units, and increased efforts by the U.S. government. The U.S. State Department alone has spent more than $100 million to protect its personnel abroad (Jack, 1976). Still, the majority of steps taken have been directed at improvements in physical security, which in turn is primarily intended to preclude indiscriminate attacks. The need persists to improve personal, individual, highly discriminate target defense.

The primary focus of any executive protection program is on the executive and the attempts to create around him areas or zones of safety. The result is a dual concept. One begins to develop aphelion and perihelion spatial concepts with respect to potential threats and their relationship to the executive.

Absolute safety is unobtainable; therefore, most security systems represent a conscious effort to create safe havens within which the executive can be expected to enjoy maximal safety. When he is inhabiting one of these havens, usually his residence or place of business, there is a general tendency on the part of security forces to relax. Because of this tendency, it is necessary that only highly reliable physical security devices be installed at these locations.

When the executive sojourns away from a safe haven, perhaps enroute to another, he enters a transitory environment precluding the installation of most conventional hardware systems. The responsibility incumbent upon the security force and the potential threat against the executive escalate almost logarithmically as the distance from the nearest haven increases.

This increasing distance often forces the abandonment of most security system components. For example, if the executive finds it necessary that he travel from the East to the West Coast, he would in all probability fly, leaving behind him the safety of the havens, the armored automobile, and the numerical superiority of the security force at the home location. Quite naturally, the security force accompanying the executive would be required to redouble their efforts and exercise a greater degree of alertness than normally required.

When one again considers the dual concept of protection, one sees that, while within a safe haven, the potential source of harm can be maintained at its greatest distance, hence the aphelion concept. Outside the haven, in a transitory environment, these sources of harm are allowed by circumstance to draw ever closer to the executive, representing the perihelion point of their orbit.

Spatial relationships between the target or executive and his would-be assailant have great impact upon the identification of the threat and the definition of methods likely to be employed. It is reasonable to assume that one wishing to do harm to another would find a greater variety of means to accomplish this if he finds himself in close proximity with his target.

If one is close enough to touch another, all weapons become viable, even the use of a knife, the most personal of all weapons. As this distance grows, the availability of potential weapons decreases. At a distance of meters, a handgun or thrown bomb would accomplish the deed; but when this distance is stretched to kilometers, only a high-powered rifle will suffice.

Another point worth noting is that there are few persons capable of placing a killing shot from great distance, particularly at a moving target. There is also the consideration of selecting a point from which to fire the weapon. One would normally be required to find a position of height, yet a position allowing the secret transport of the rifle. The required height to achieve the proper angle of fire also increases the time required to make good an escape and reduces the available escape routes. The assailant must first reach ground level before he can flee.

In the majority of cases involving assassination, the attack has been made from close quarters, using a handgun, and from a height nearly identical to that of the target. Richard Lawrence, in his unsuccessful attempt upon President Andrew Jackson in 1835, was standing but a scant six feet away. Had it not been for his pistol's double misfire, Jackson would have become the first United States President to have been assassinated (Morison, 1962).

John Wilkes Booth was also at the same height as

Lincoln when he shot the President in 1865 (Whitney, 1969). Garfield, in 1881, also was shot at close range by his assailant Charles Guiteau. Attempts upon Franklin Roosevelt, the assassination of Robert Kennedy, and most others were also at close range and with handguns.

John Kennedy was an exception to this rule. Lee Harvey Oswald was on the sixth floor of the Texas School Book Depository and fired down on the President as he motored along Dealy Plaza (Manchester, 1967). This assassination was unique also in that Oswald did not have to stalk Kennedy; the target came to the assassin. This does, however, underline the dangers inherent to the transitory environment.

In seeking to establish safe havens, one will find beneficial the many excellent books dealing with physical security. Moolman's (1970) book concerning residential security is but one example. In this effort, one will find outlined the concepts of establishing safe-rooms and security landscaping. Also discussed is the variety of locking devices available. They are treated in terms of primary and secondary systems, terms also common in Roper (1976). Roper details the mechanical intricacies of both simple and complex locking devices in such a manner as to allow the reader to arrive at intelligent decisions concerning quality and price. He includes a detailed explanation of "mastering" systems and key controls. Additional expertise in the field of residential security, particularly with respect to perimeter lighting techniques, has been made available by Griffin (1975).

Alarm systems are a must in both the professional and residential environments. One must realize that there is nothing new in the concept of alarm utilization, a practice dating back to 390 B.C. when the Romans employed squawking geese to alert them of a surprise attack by the Gauls (National Advisory Committee on Criminal Justice Standards and Goals, 1976). The complexity of current systems demands that the designer of a protection system look carefully and critically at both the weaknesses and strengths of alarm models. It has been alleged that "In today's marketplace, the consumer is better able to select the correct lawnmower than obtain the proper private security services" (National Advisory Committee, 1976, p. 243).

The problems of false alarms generating erroneous reactions and adquate power systems to insure continued protection during periods of public service failures both demand attention. One can find available many valuable publications dealing with this issue (General Services Administration, PBS, P 5930.2A, 1970).

❧ Finally, one must realize that security is a total product; it is not found only in stronger locks and thicker doors. The most modern of components utilizing the most esoteric electronic wizardry is rendered useless in the hands of incompetent personnel. Preemployment screening of prospective security personnel to insure capability and trustworthiness is critical (National Advisory Committee, 1976).

The cost of security can often be much less than the final cost of terrorism. The FBI reported that 42 persons were killed, 242 injured, and $23.4 million in property damage resulted from 1,574 bombing incidents in the first nine months of 1975 (FBI National Bomb Center Reports, 1975).

Summary

There are no claims that the establishment of an executive protection system is easy or inexpensive, only that it is a subject worthy of serious corporate consideration. There are many references available that serve to increase understanding of specific areas of security. The difficulty lies in the absence of a whole concept approach, especially in the area of executive protection.

Given time, an experienced security manager can accomplish the necessary research into the various aspects dealing with security hardware systems. He can amass information pertaining to risk management and then set about outlining the specific design he deems suitable for his corporation. This task can require many months of effort, depending upon his experience and expertise. After expending the time, the designer is still faced with the actual design of his protective service.

This guide is intended to provide the advice required to allow the security designer-manager to begin his personalized design, resorting to additional research only in those facets of security of which he is unsure. If nothing more, it should allow implementation of a new protective system months earlier than would normally be expected. The saving of months can well mean the saving of lives within the corporation.

In the following chapter, we will begin consideration of the design of the security system. The first topics to be examined will be those of the administrative policy involving the size of the security section and the level of its management. The second area within this chapter will deal with organizational policy. An attempt will be made to determine which corporations require executive protection and to ascertain the identity of those within these corporations who require protective service. Also discussed will be the determination of the degree of protection to be afforded.

CHAPTER 4

Administrative Policy

Divisional Size

THE final size of the security division is a product of the overall scope of its responsibility. No attempt will be made to determine the numerical size of an executive protection system. There are, however, other considerations imposed by size. The first of these is the actual organizational composition of the division.

It is clear that delegation and decentralization are desirable in most organizations, but only with adequate controls. These controls begin with staffing the division. Continuous control is achieved through structure and supervision. The security division should be structured according to function.

The environments of the executive, the professional, residential, and transitory, have been previously discussed. The first functional segregation of the security division occurs in these areas of responsibility. Because of the extensive overlap, it is better that the residential and transitory environments be consolidated into a single segment. The professional environment, normally the plant, corporate headquarters, and so on, is considered as the second functional segregation or segment within the security division.

To these we add two other segments, the technical services section and an investigative-intelligence section, bringing the total to four functional units within the executive protection service.

The responsibility of the residential-transitory section would be the provision of protective coverage to the executive(s) in his home or apartment and during periods of travel. The men assigned to this section would be required to travel in advance of and with the executive when his corporate duties take him out of town. It would be their responsibility to coordinate the movements of the executive with the other sections to insure continuity of protection.

The professional environment section would be responsible for plant security and for the protection of executives while in their area. This section would incorporate uniformed guards. No other section would do so.

Technical services would be responsible for the hardware utilized by all other units and would provide communications and technical expertise to these other sections as required. In addition, technical services would also implement security surveys of all environments, insuring the continuous effective protection of all executives and the proper operation of security equipment.

The final section is that of investigations and intelligence. The responsibility of this group would be to gather intelligence upon which updating of the threat analysis would be based. These individuals would also have the primary responsibility for effective liaison between the security service and local law enforcement agencies. Preemployment personal security investigations and the resolution of any allegations concerning security or corporate employees would also be the responsibility of the investigations and intelligence segment.

With the exception of the technical services section, it would be advantageous periodically to rotate personnel from section to section, insuring that functional knowledge of all areas is gained by all personnel. Nonrotation of technical security personnel is based upon the technical qualifications required by those assigned to this section. Technical services personnel should receive training in the other sections in addition to their own specialty.

Level of Management

The major thrust of this guide thus far has been in the establishment of an entity termed the executive protection service. To insure that this new corporate division functions properly, one must examine the issue of placement within the organizational structure.

In essence, one is asking the question "At what level within the system will the security manager function?" The need for autonomy coupled with the potential requirement for rapid approval of ideas demanding immediate implementation and the required authority during crisis situations dictate that this position not be subservient to another, with the obvious exception of the chief executive of the corporation.

If, for example, the security manager is placed below a staff function on the organizational chart, he must function through his superior who, in turn, would be required to function through his superior, who himself is subordinate to the chief executive.

Organizational charts are representative of corporate lines of authority, and traditionally, this authority is observed. In an emergency situation, it is unlikely that an individual at the staff level would possess the authority to approve unique action. It is doubtful that he would exercise the initiative to assume this authority. Townsend (1970) declared that for each succeeding level on an organizational chart, there is a corresponding loss of efficiency up to 25 percent. Security efficiency, particularly during times of crisis, can ill afford a loss.

It is not realistic to envision management of the security division at the executive level of the chart; therefore, it is possibly best to consider placing this position outside the direct lines of authority. The security division should occupy a position independent of all executive positions save that of the chief executive (Fig. 1).

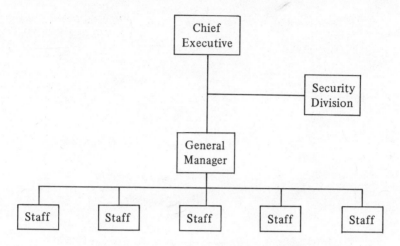

Figure 1. Suggested Organizational Chart

Commenting on the various conventional organizational charts, Townsend (1970) suggested employment of a somewhat unusual system, the circular organization. Townsend described the more conventional charts as being demoralizing, since nobody thinks of himself as being beneath other people. In the better organizations, people see themselves as occupying equally important positions, as if they were seated at a round table. One of these positions would be defined as that of leader simply because someone has to make the tactical decisions that enable the organization to keep functioning.

The circular organization illustrated in Figure 2 represents the functional divisions of a security section. The security manager is defined as such, and the separate supervisors are depicted in the major circle. In turn, security personnel assigned to the separate sections are also in a

Figure 2. Circular Organization

circular formation. In Figure 3, Townsend's comments concerning conventional charts are illustrated.

Organizational Policy

To Protect or Not

"Does this organization truly require a system of executive protection?" This is probably the first question to arise and one that is impossible to answer outside the environment in which it is posed. This question, and its ultimate answer, must be formulated by the very group

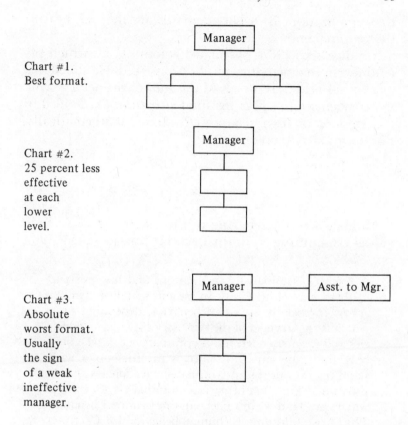

Chart #1.
Best format.

Chart #2.
25 percent less
effective
at each
lower
level.

Chart #3.
Absolute
worst format.
Usually
the sign
of a weak
ineffective
manager.

Figure 3. Townsend's Organizational Charts

which, if the answer is affirmative, would be most affected. The necessity for and merits of a protective system must first be recognized by the executive level of the corporation to which it is to be applied. The decision demands objective examination in seeking the answer. Objectivity is an elusive quality when the topic is so personal.

The expertise required to implement protective services may be found outside the organization, but the ultimate decision to implement rests entirely with the directors of the organization. By what standards are they to measure the requirement?

Abrahamsen (1967) postulated a formula by which potential criminal activities might be assessed. He stated that a criminal act (*C*) represented the sum of the actor's criminal tendencies (*T*) plus his total situation (*S*), divided by the amount of his resistance (*R*). Stated mathematically, this formula is represented as:

$$C = \frac{T + S}{R}$$

Abrahamsen was referring to the likelihood of an individual committing a criminal act. He further stated (1967, pp. 37-38):

> A person's criminalistic inclinations and his resistance to them may either result in an anti-social or criminal act or in socially approved behavior, depending upon which is the stronger of the two. All people have tendencies and countertendencies. A criminal act can take place only if the person's resistance is insufficient to withstand the pressure of his criminalistic tendencies and the situation. This mathematical formula is a concept which can be used in understanding criminal behavior. Thus if we substitute *H* (human behavior) for *C* (crime), we arrive at the same formula.

While Abrahamsen's formula is a somewhat abstract concept and not intended to convey connotations of mathematical precision with which one can absolutely predict the occurrence of a criminal act or the identity of the actor, it does provide a viable tool for understanding deviate behavior. Through a modification of Abrahamsen's formula, one can create a guide synergetic to the original problem: Is a protective service system required by a specific concern?

Suppose one substitutes the letters *Po,* representing the term probability of occurrence, for Abrahamsen's *C* or *H*? One then has the equation:

$$Po = \frac{T+S}{R}$$

In this modification, one is not concerned with the antisocial potential of an individual, but with the potential threat to a corporation and its executives. Tendency (*T*), now becomes trend, the historical actions of radical groups and the history of violence directed at the corporation and other like corporations. It also concerns the past history of those groups that are identified as being active within the immediate locale.

Situations (*S*), now refers to the current socioeconomic and political conditions with which the corporation is linked. These factors encompass labor situations of under- and unemployment, foreign contracts, and the present level of activity on the part of surrounding groups. For example, a concern involved in the production of instruments of warfare, whose major sales in recent times were to South Africa and whose physical plant was located in an inner-city area heavily populated with blacks, might well be considered to rate a high hypothetical number within the *S* section of the formula.

The final factor within the formula is that of resistance (*R*) and is intended to represent that amount of resistance that the perpetrator of an assault or kidnapping plot is likely to encounter. It involves the critical assessment of local law enforcement agencies and the amount of sympathy within the community directed toward those most likely to attempt such action. Resistance and probability of occutrence (*Po*) are inversely proportional.

While other methods certainly exist with which one might evaluate the need for executive protection, any valid system must take into consideration those factors previously indicated. In reality, the decision of whether or not to incorporate a system of executive protection would probably be self-evident. One is unlikely to consider or seek protection unless one feels in some way threatened.

Assuming that our answer is "Yes, this organization is in need of an effective system of executive protection," one can then turn to the second issue, namely, that of identifying those to be protected.

Who Is To Be Protected?

This is perhaps the single most difficult decision required by the design of an executive protection system. If one wished to state the problem in a negative way, one is choosing whom not to protect. Economic considerations preclude the extension of this service to every member of the corporation; even the most affluent of companies could not afford such measures.

The selection of one individual over another to receive protection does not imply that one man's life is more valuable than another. Morally, all men might be considered equal; realistically, however, there are those whose talents and abilities make them more valuable within a certain context. The decision to protect these men should represent the result of a painstaking and objective evaluation of the risks involved and the impact upon the corporation in the event that these individuals should be lost.

Criddle (1964, p. 25) described the loss impact of an executive by posing a personal axiom:

> Whenever any vital corporate function is dependent upon the personal qualifications of any unique individ-

ual(s), a risk exists with respect to the loss of services, and an unfavorable outcome results in economic loss.

Prior to discussion of *how* one makes the needed decision, it is imperative that another issue be examined, that of *who* makes the determination of which individuals are to be protected.

It is difficult, if not impossible, for absolutely objective decisions to be reached by individuals having a high emotional investment in the topic under examination. For this reason, it would be unrealistic for the members of the board or executive committee to determine the recipients of protective services among themselves.

Contrary to the common belief that committees are typically cautious, compromising, and conservative, group decisions are more risky than are individual decisions. Authority for decisions in a business enterprise should therefore be given to a responsible individual rather than to a group (Rim, 1964).

This is not to suggest that the security manager or designer make this determination. It is very doubtful that the authority of this individual would be that broad. It can safely be assumed that the corporate director, president, or whichever individual is located at the apex of the bureaucratic structure would himself receive executive protection. This man, acting upon the advice of the security manager, and after all factors involving risk have been analyzed, should be the individual making the final determination.

It should be understood by all that protection is extended to a corporate position, not to the individual. By this it is meant that should an executive be the foreign manager for a corporation in an area where kidnapping is epidemic, for example Italy, this individual might well receive protective service. The selection would be based upon the position and current situation. Should this executive be transferred into another area where little or no risk existed, the protective service would then be extended to his successor.

Redlick (1968) proposed that every risk was quantifiable and that quantifiability of risk ranged from computation to estimate. This might well be true; however, risk is also multidimension, and so, there exist individual differences in perception of risk and differences in reaction to that perceived risk (Slovic, 1964).

The evaluation of various corporate positions must be accomplished in the most realistic and objective manner possible. If not, the resultant advice, upon which the corporate leader must base his decisions, would be misleading and dangerous.

Two separate risk classifications have been established: speculative and pure (Mowbray and Blanchard, 1955). The significant distinction between them is that speculative risk — investments, business ventures, gambling — may have an outcome that produces either profit or loss, whereas the outcome of pure risk is loss or no loss. In the field of the executive, one dealing only with pure risk, the goal is the achievement of a no-loss posture. Corporate loss is represented by the kidnapping, assassination, and bombing with injury of a corporate executive, a far greater loss than that experienced in speculative risk situations.

As previously mentioned, prior to determination regarding the identification of the specific individuals who are to receive protection, an analysis of risk or potential of occurrence of an undesirable event must be accomplished for each separate corporate position. In analyzing each corporate position, one is well advised to draw a position profile (Fig. 4), a chart reflecting the existing threat of kidnapping, bombing, and assassination in each of the three environments.

	Professional	Transitory	Residential	TOTALS
Kidnapping				
Bombing				
Assassination				
TOTALS				

Figure 4. Position Profile Chart

After examining the probabilities that one or more of the three events might occur in each of the environments, one can develop a foundation upon which to base recommendations for executive protection.

Houston (1964, pp. 511-12) has described three types of probability:

1. A priori: Probability that is deducible from the nature of a situation, i.e., the probability of getting a one when throwing a six-sided die
2. Statistical: Probability that can be arrived at inductively by examining a large number of observations, i.e., the probability that a twenty-year-old man will die in the next year
3. Estimate or judgement: Probability that cannot be determined objectively but can only be believed intuitively, i.e., the probability that a new restaurant in a neighborhood will be profitable

It can now be seen that one is dealing in an area of pure risk where the probability of undesirable occurrence must primarily be based upon estimate or judgement, a highly tenuous position indeed.

One method for quantifying the requirement for protection is through the assignment of numerical values or weight to specific factors. The first of these factors is that of the probability of occurrence of a specific event..

Probability of occurrence (Po) is arrived at through an extensive analysis of the statistical record of past losses affecting a particular organization over a specified period of time. After such an analysis, the probability of a specific event occurring in a particular environment should be assigned a numerically expressed weight. This numerical value is an arbitrary figure. For our purposes, we will assume that the number ranges from 1 to 10. No zero value can be assigned because one cannot state, absolutely, that the occurrence of a specific event is impossible. On this scale, the value 10 would represent or indicate that the event will surely occur. The value 1 represents that in all probability the event will not occur.

The second factor is that of impact (I) upon the corporation in terms of maximum probable loss and maximum possible loss should the event occur. This factor would depend upon which position was being profiled and the presence or absence of unique circumstances, for example, that the occupant of the position possesses knowledge no other executive has access to. The numerical value attached to the impact factor will range from 10 to 100. No zero value is used in this factor since the loss of any executive through an incident of violence would automatically have some impact upon the corporation. Higher values are selected since impact, or loss, is the primary motivating factor in the establishment of protective services and therefore carries greater weight.

If the loss of a particular individual would result in prolonged interruption to corporate activities and a substantial dollar loss, the numerical value assigned might approach 100. If, on the other hand, the impact to the corporation were estimated to be a minimal dollar loss and no interruption in operation, the resultant impact value might best be represented as 10.

The final factor is that of predictability (P). This represents the most subjective category of the three factors, so extreme care should be exercised in the assignment of a numerical value. These values will range from 1 to 10, with the value of 1 representative of the inability to predict the occurrence of an event. Conversely, 10 would represent the event as being absolutely predictable. No zero base is assigned to this factor since it would be impossible to divide a number by zero, and thereby our formula would be mathematically inoperable.

An example of predictability is the occurrence of a large number of kidnappings in a country with a long history of kidnappings. One could predict that the trend is unlikely to continue. If there were to occur a sudden spate of kidnappings in an area with no past history of such acts and little were known about the current events, predictability would be very low.

Risk was previously defined as the variation in the possible outcomes that exist in nature in a given situation. When risk is high, the ability to predict the future is low and vice versa. Risk is the mathematical product obtained by multiplying the probability of occurrence (Po) by the impact (I).

If then this resultant risk is divided by predictability (P), one arrives at a figure that is representative of the threat, the threat assessment (Ta). These factors can be expressed mathematically as follows:

$$Po \bullet I = R \quad \text{and} \quad \frac{R}{P} = Ta$$

To illustrate an application of the above formulae, assume that one is examining the risk posed to a corporate executive by the threat of kidnapping. Further hypothesize that this executive is a scientist working on a very complex chemical product and is the sole person within the corporation with a complete knowledge of the project. If this man were to be kidnapped, the research project would cease immediately. In the event that he were not returned safely, it would require a minimum of five months for another scientist to duplicate the work to date. This represents a considerable impact upon the corporation, so one would assign a high impact value, let us assume the figure of 80.

Assume now that the scientist is residing and working in an area where kidnappings have occurred with a frequency of several each year for a number of years, these prior kidnappings being the work of a terrorist organization that is still active. One can assess the probability of occurrence value for the transitory environment at a value of 6. This represents a relatively high assessment. If one were assessing the *Po* for the professional environment, with its inherently greater numbers of security personnel, the value would be approximately 2.

Applying our first equation ($Po \bullet I = R$), a risk factor or quotient of 480 has been established. Now, in order that one might establish a threat assessment (Ta), one must determine predictability (P).

Since the kidnappings for our hypothetical area have been continuous in nature, the groups operating in the area have become well-known and their leadership identified. One assumes that, in this case, good liaison with the local agencies has been practiced. By this means, we are well informed of terrorist activities and, occasionally, their plans. We now have a situation in which predictability is relatively high, so one assigns a value of 7.

Recalling that risk divided by predictability equals our derived threat assessment, one has now arrived at a figure, an evaluation of the risk of kidnapping in a transitory environment, of 68.6. These computations must be accomplished for each environment and for each threat: kidnapping, bombing, and assassination. Examination of a completed position profile (Fig. 5) reflects in which environment each threat poses the greatest problem in the design of the protective system.

	Professional	Transitory	Residential	TOTALS
Kidnapping	26.4	68.6	52.5	147.5
Bombing	28.1	73	64.2	165.3
Assassination	30	75	69.5	174.5
TOTALS	84.5	216.6	186.2	487.3

Figure 5. Completed Position Profile Chart

The foregoing discussion has been an attempt to quantify risk and thereby divorce the identification of those to be protected from an emotional arena. This also will provide a basis for several other design factors within the protective service. This is by no means an implication that the method discussed is *the* way to achieve quantification, only that it is one way. Reflective, experienced security designers should be able to weigh the needs of their particular organization and arrive at variations to this approach to the problem.

Degree of Protection

The degree or level of protection offered can best be classified under one of two extremes: that of high profile or that of low profile. These profiles are very flexible, and seldom would one executive receive a single degree of protection in all environments. To provide high profile in all environments would involve a strategy of maximum security, a hard line of defensive measures for the executive and his family at all times and all locations. An example of such protection would be that extended to the President of the United States of America and to his family.

High profile protection is extremely visible, involving a maximum use of hardware in the residential, transitory, and professional environments. This degree of protection would include, but not be limited to, a protected compound within which the executive would reside. The compound would be equipped with highly sophisticated technology and live-in body guards. It would also incorporate several lines of defense, utilizing specially trained dogs on the grounds and within the quarters.

High profile would also involve armed transportation, armored-type vehicles, and drivers trained in evasive and defensive driving techniques. Extensive communications would be employed, tying the executive to the security center at all times. Defensive training might well include a policy of "kill to protect."

Within the professional environment, this policy would utilize restrictive controls over movement throughout the facility. Both continous and stationary guards at key positions would be employed, and there would exist strategically located "panic" buttons enabling the executive to summon protective personnel at a moment's notice. There might be built into both office and residence safe-rooms into which the executive and his family could retire during emergencies. Additionally, under this concept, the kidnapped executive could expect his company to enter into no negotiations nor pay any ransom demands on behalf of him or his family.

At the opposite end of the spectrum, one finds the low profile approach. Roughly the opposite in philosophy and application as that described above, the low profile approach calls for a minimum of security in the form of personnel and hardware. Instead, it is a system whereby avoidance of risk is stressed.

In developing position profiles, one arrives at a numerical value termed the threat assessment. When risks are identified and assessed, it is the function of security services to reduce these conditions. Generally, there are five types of risk reduction (Shackle, 1961, p. 267):

1. Risk avoidance: Attempting to remove the executive from, or lower his exposure to, locations and periods of risk
2. Occurrence reduction: Attempting to reduce the activities during which the executive will be threatened
3. Risk acceptance: Allowing a risk or threat to exist due to one's inability to deal with it, but with an intensified monitoring of that risk
4. Risk spreading: Simply by assigning functions to multiple individuals so that the corporate impact upon loss is reduced
5. Risk transference: Use of insurance programs to transfer the dollar liability for the loss to another party

In the case of terrorist acts, frequently involving the loss of lives, the first three methods are most frequently employed. So it is with low profile that one would stress the first technique.

Avoidance may, in a low profile strategy, attempt to camouflage the identity of the executive by causing him to blend into his surroundings and to render the appearance that he is one of the ordinary employees rather than an executive.

In low profile situations, the executive's home would not be found within the walls of a compound, and it would employ few, if any, servants and little security hardware. Conventional means of physical security would be utilized: strong locks, a fire detection system, and perhaps glazed glass to hamper the throwing of bombs into the home.

Under this system, the executive and his family members would be educated and trained to employ conventional precautionary measures. For example, he would drive himself to and from work in a common type of vehicle, far from being ostentatious. The executive would be taught to vary his routes and departure times but not to engage in violent resistive measures.

The corporate policy in this case might well be one of negotiation and the payment of reasonable hostage demands. If this is to be the policy, it would benefit the corporation to employ the fifth method of risk reduction, that of obtaining kidnap and ransom insurance covering the executive and his family.

The level of protection need not be consistent. In certain instances, an executive might receive low profile within the professional environment, high profile while in transit, and a blend of the two in his residence.

The cost of implementing high profile protection obviously exceeds that of low profile. It would be impossible to ascertain the cost, even an estimate, without a complete understanding of the total situation. Still, cost considerations are important. Technological hardware advancements over the past few years currently offer the security manager or designer options and cost savings that were not available before. The following concepts might be considered:

1. Portable intrusion alarm systems installed at the executive's home might well aid in the reduction of total manpower requirements.
2. Use of night viewing devices and equipment can reduce the total number of security personnel required during a night shift.
3. Use of covert communications equipment and duress alarms can provide additional security while enhancing the executive's privacy and also reducing manpower requirements.
4. Use of specially trained dogs and handlers can often reduce the number of men required.
5. Many items of equipment purchased for one security application might well be employed in other modes through careful preplanning and improve the total system. An item of optical equipment might prove useful as part of a closed circuit television system, a night viewing device, or a photographic surveillance system.
6. The same approach to manpower utilization may provide for more cost-effective security. Funds spent for training of drivers in techniques of defensive driving might make it possible to eliminate the need for an escort vehicle and driver during routine executive movement.

Having completed the first three critical steps in the design of an executive protection system, those of identification of corporate and individual need for protection and the determination of the degree of protection required, one must now examine the issues of operational policy.

CHAPTER 5

Operational Policy

Use of Force

FORCE is defined as a strength used against a person or thing. It is also defined as the power of control or influence over others. From these definitions it can be seen that force is a concept of considerable scope. It can range from verbal coercion to the taking of a life.

Since force obviously cannot be considered as a constant, the key word governing its application would be *apposite*. Understandably, the appositeness of force would vary with the conditions demanding its formulation. If, for example, a demonstrator were shouting obscenities at a corporate executive, a security guard would hardly have cause to shoot him. If, on the other hand, this same demonstrator were to point a weapon at the executive, the guard would hopefully respond with stronger measures than shouting "Stop!"

The idea is, of course, to apply just that degree of force made necessary by the circumstances, no more and no less. It is imperative that protection personnel understand that their primary purpose is not to "get the attacker" but to save the executive.

This means that if a crisis situation were to arise in which deadly force were required in order to save the executive from possible loss of life or serious injury, this degree of force would be warranted. If, however, it is possible to remove the executive from this danger without directing force at another, then the first consideration must be toward this removal.

In utilizing that amount of force necessary to save the life of the executive or to prevent his injury, once the danger is past and the situation is under control, additional employment of force would not be allowed. One would not be compelled to release an attacker once the executive is removed to a place of safety; he would of course be held for the authorities. One simply would no longer have justification for overly aggressive acts. It would be wise for the security manager to insure that proper use of force is clearly understood by all security personnel and for him to remove promptly any individual who shows a proclivity toward violence.

There is a moral contract on the part of the corporation, obligating the organization to support security personnel in the event that legal action is taken against them following the performance of their duties. The corporation is obligated to provide legal services and, in the event of a judgement against an individual guard, to pay all cost incurred.

Relationship With External Agencies

There is no substitute for good liaison with other agencies. Through careful cultivation of relationships with members of local and state law enforcement agencies, the security manager and his staff can enhance their operation immeasurably. These relationships must be founded upon mutual respect and trust and must incorporate shared intelligence. The security manager who attempts to use others, constantly seeking but never rendering information, will soon find his efforts rebuffed. It is of particular importance that the supervisor of the investigative and intelligence section of the program actively seek to establish rapport with others in security and law enforcement.

In the event that a kidnapping occurs, it is often the case that precipitate release of the news might foster adverse conditions with respect to the safe return of the victim.

Good liaison will more often than not insure that this does not occur.

To assist in developing the desired relationships, it might be advisable that a special fund be established in the security program budget to cover the cost of such expenditures as luncheons, dinners, and token awards for affable competitions between staff and local agencies, for example, marksmanship, basketball, golf, and so on. All of these items serve to bring personnel together and stimulate the growth of friendships. It could prove beneficial at these functions to include among the guests-competitors particular members of the press, specifically those reporters who cover law enforcement and city courts and are familiar with criminal conditions in the area. This is by no means an attempt to compromise the press; it simply is availing oneself of potentially valuable contacts.

Investigations and Intelligence

Not only must the security manager use all legal and ethical means of gathering information about threats to his organization, but he must also shield that organization against those who would engage in espionage. The collection responsiblity for an executive protection system is best accomplished by a dedicated unit whose sole responsibility lies in the realm of investigations and intelligence (I & I) operations. This unit should concentrate its collection efforts in four specific areas:

1. Information on groups and individuals that are known or suspected to be specific threats against the organization
2. Analysis of patterns, trends, and relationships of terrorists, criminals, and advocates of civil unrest
3. Dissemination of information to security and management personnel for strengthening the preventive aspects of the security program

4. Protection of the organization from penetration by terrorists, criminals, and advocates of civil unrest

It would be the responsibility of I & I to create an information resource that would actively and accurately produce objective information for security use. This information also would prove useful as a medium of mutual cooperation between the security division and local, state, and federal agencies.

Earlier it was suggested that rotation of security personnel between the separate sections within the executive protection service might be useful. At that time it was pointed out that the unique requirements of the technical service section exempted its personnel from rotation; to some degree this holds true for the I & I section as well.

Within I & I, those individuals functioning as investigators would primarily be conducting personnel security investigations and therefore be subject to rotational utilization. Their function is an overt activity, and they would become well-known throughout the community as a result. In conducting background investigations this is an advantage.

Operations of an intelligence nature are often conducted clandestinely or by covert means, and the investigators accomplishing this are better off if they maintain a low profile, that is, they are not quite so visible. Therefore, rotation within this group should be done sparingly if at all.

No clandestine or covert operation should be undertaken without complete prior knowledge of the security manager. These types of activities must be monitored closely and not utilized excessively.

Hostage Policy

While it is the ultimate goal of any executive protection service to provide protection, as the title implies, failures must be anticipated and prepared for. There should be contingency plans designed to be implemented in the event of a crisis. This means the existence of a well-defined and clearly understood hostage policy. With respect to hostage policies, there are but two options: to pay ransom or not.

If it is to be the official policy of the corporation not to enter into negotiations or pay ransom demands, this policy should be understood by the executives within the firm. It would not be a bad idea if it unofficially became well-known outside the corporation as well.

Because the corporate mind is subject to rapid change, the security manager should, regardless of the corporate policy concerning hostage policy, formulate a crisis plan that would include the designation of responsibility, identity of executives covered by the plan, and implementation criteria for the plan. The security manager should maintain an emergency biographical data folder for each of the identified executives. This information should be gathered and maintained under strict security, perhaps allowing the executives to complete the forms themselves, place them in envelopes, and seal them prior to giving them to the security manager. This folder should contain the following information (Private Security Advisory Council, 1976):

1. Recent color photographs of the executive and his family
2. Signature cards and fingerprint cards
3. Reel-to-reel voice tapes, recorded at speeds of not less than 7 1/2 ips
4. Biographical information to include
   a. Complete names
   b. All residences
   c. Physical descriptions
   d. Bank account identification and credit card

numbers
- e. Names of physicians, dentists, and opticians
- f. Automobile identification of all vehicles
- g. Listing of relatives and addresses
- h. Listing of clubs, hobbies, and other activities

If corporate policy is to be one of negotiation with kidnappers, it would be wise to consider kidnap and ransom (K & R) insurance. In the past three years, there have been more than 775 kidnappings in the United States, with ransom demands of at least $28 million. An insurance expert with Lloyd's of London, the leader in the field of K & R, reports that the company has issued thousands of policies. This type of insurance can be secured from several United States companies as well (Berger, 1978).

K & R insurance is designed to reimburse the insured for money paid in a legitimate kidnapping. The insurance companies do not advance the money with which the demands are paid. The insurance agency also retains "first recovery" rights. The policy is usually a deductible type. If, for example, ransom in the amount of $3 million were paid, the insured would pay the first portion of the ransom, perhaps 33 percent. This means that the corporation would pay the $3 million and then be reimbursed $2 million. If the kidnappers were apprehended and a portion of the money recovered, the insurance company would recover their loss first. Any money over that amount would be returned to the corporation.

The cost of K & R insurance varies with the location of the executives who are to be insured, the type of corporation seeking the insurance, and the security program utilized by the corporation. Some corporations are too well-known and certain individuals are too famous to be insured. If insurance is issued, its continuation is dependent upon the maintenance of secrecy concerning its existence. For comparative purposes, consider that a policy covering four top executives working in Argentina for an American firm would cost $112,500 per year for total coverage of $5 million. This same policy in the United States would cost only $2,750.

Crisis Plan

No program of executive protection is complete until a very thorough crisis plan is formulated. Regardless of elaborate protection schemes, the security manager must realize that a failure can occur, an executive could be kidnapped. Even though the official corporate policy might be one of "no negotiation," it must be understood that this policy is subject to last minute change. The security manager must be prepared for this event and have a well-designed crisis plan on standby.

This plan should be detailed, it should be understood with absolute clarity by the members of the crisis team, and it should be closely guarded. Members of the crisis team should be named in the plan and their functions delineated. It is this team that would deal with the ensuing series of events following a kidnapping.

The team should consist of no more than four members; to have more could create confusion in a circumstance where faultlessness is demanded. Ideally the members of the crisis team should include the following individuals:

1. Coordinator: Preferably the security manager, whose function is to implement the crisis plan. He should be the single person informing the top decision makers within the corporation.
2. Assistant to the coordinator: Ideally the supervisor of the I & I section, since his knowledge of terrorist groups and current situations should be the most comprehensive. This individual should be familiar with every aspect of the crisis plan.
3. Technical advisor: Logically, the supervisor of the

technical services section of security. His function is to implement all technical countermeasures, e.g., telephone taps to provide voice recordings, communications, and other such requirements.

4. Legal counsel: Primarily present to answer corporate legal questions and to insure that any needed legal documents are prepared correctly.

The crisis plan also should identify specific equipment required for an emergency. It should provide a checklist of all the mechanics of establishing a crisis operations center. This list would preclude inadvertently overlooking some detail.

A record or log should be started immediately upon implementaiton of the crisis plan and should be highly detailed. All telephone conversations involving the crisis operations center should be recorded.

Only one individual should communicate with the kidnappers following the establishment of communications with them. Initial contact will most likely occur by telephone, and while tracing telephone calls is a technical possibility, it is a time-consuming task and should not be depended upon to any great degree. This technique is far better suited to motion picture and television drama than to real-life crisis.

It is far more important that the crisis team maintain a communications link with the kidnappers than stall for time, hoping for a phone trace, and risk causing the kidnappers to terminate all communications. There are certain steps that the crisis team members must take during the initial contact with the kidnappers.

The kidnappers should be given a recognition code, perhaps a key word and number. This code must be held in secrecy, as it will allow the crisis team positively to identify the caller during future conversations. It is not unheard of for individuals other than the actual kidnapper to attempt to extort ransom payment once a kidnapping becomes well-known.

A variation of this technique of identification is the provision of a series of key words to each executive. A duplicate listing would be maintained in the biographical file of that executive within the security section. The kidnapped executive could point out to his abductors that he must provide a different code for each contact. If threatened into providing the entire list, the executive could provide this list out of sequence and thereby alert the security manager that he is under duress.

It is important that the individual dealing with the kidnapper continue to do so, that there not be several changes of negotiator that would hamper efforts to establish rapport. The negotiator need not be the security manager, although this situation would have definite advantages. He should possess the following characteristics:

1. Good physical condition
2. Mature appearance
3. Good speaking voice
4. Excellent verbal skills of interrogator
5. Be patient
6. Be a member of an ethnic or racial group (depending upon the circumstances)
7. Be a volunteer for the assignment

During all negotiations, attempts should be made to slow the proceedings down, and patience and self-control must be exercised. The more time one can gain, the more likely it is that the crisis will end with no loss of life. The negotiator should never promise anything that he cannot deliver; he should never portray himself as being the ultimate decision maker. It is good policy not to make any promise without first extracting a promise in return. This promise on the part of the kidnappers need not be anything of great importance; it simply establishes a pattern of give and take.

While the negotiator should not promise what he cannot deliver, he also should not make a categorical refusal to demands. It is better to point out that certain demands cannot be complied with, that there must be some basis for agreement and the safe return of the executive.

Even in instances when the corporation is willing to meet the initial demands, attempts should be made to negotiate lower terms. This will prevent scaring the kidnappers into thinking that some form of entrapment is planned. During the negotiations, one should also attempt to extract reasonable guarantees as to when and where the executive will be returned and an agreement that acceptance of the kidnapper's demands will mean that no further extortion threats will be made.

In making payment, special preparations should be made; the serial numbers of the money should be recorded and, in some cases, special dyes can be applied. The FBI suggests that they prepare the ransom money, but the security system negotiator should be the one to make delivery of the money.

During negotiations, the kidnappers should be advised that the negotiator will be armed when he makes delivery of the ransom money. It should be explained that this is a simple precaution against his being robbed while carrying the cash. It is far better to let the kidnappers know that he will be armed than to have this come as a surprise during delivery.

Following the safe return of the executive, he should be thoroughly debriefed, and a full and complete account of the event should be recorded as soon as possible. Advance training of the executive will prove invaluable should he be kidnapped. This topic, along with environmental design, will be discussed in the following chapter.

CHAPTER 6

Design

Environmental Design

THE cardinal sin of any protective effort is underestimating the opposition. Terrorists are not stupid. They employ methods of assessing their targets that are as sophisticated as those of the security force. They are capable of detecting weaknesses, if they exist, in any security system and incorporate multiple techniques to gather information concerning an intended target. Often these include surveillances, pretext calls and visits, subverting of employees, and many other efforts.

Sir Geoffrey Jackson stated that for six months prior to his kidnapping, he had been the object of surveillance at his home and at the embassy. He was surveyed by individuals on motor scooters, by families of picnickers near his residence, and by couples embracing near the embassy (Jackson, 1974).

Once satisfied that they have gathered adequate intelligence, the terrorists will determine the time, place, and method of their action. It is the responsibility of the executive protection service to effectively counter these efforts. It is imperative that highly professional security measures be designed and implemented in each of the three environments. Security must recognize the methods of action employed by terrorists and which of these methods is most likely to be utilized in each environment.

Marighella, representing the essence of terrorist thought, listed fourteen methods of action to be directed against vulnerable targets (1971, p. 97):

1. Attack
2. Entry or break-in
3. Ambush
4. Occupation
5. Tactical street fighting
6. Theft of arms, ammunition, and explosives
7. Liberation of prisoners
8. Execution
9. Sabotage
10. Bombings
11. Strikes and other work disruptions
12. Armed propaganda
13. Kidnapping
14. The war of nerves

The following examination of the residential, transitory, and professional environments is formulated largely in terms of Marighella's strategy.

Residential Environment

The residence emerges as a primary terrorist target for two reasons: First, it is a center of activity. The executive leaves and returns here, his family is located here, and much of his corporate activity occurs here. Second, the residence is vulnerable to nine of Marighella's methods of action: attack, entry or break-in, ambush, occupation, execution, sabotage, bombing, kidnapping, and the war of nerves.

Attacks and entry methods of attack are most likely to take place under cover of darkness. The success of the attack depends upon it being swift and merciless. Alarms are ignored and no attempt is made to disable or bypass them, the theory being that the attack is over before assistance arrives. Servants and residual guard forces are shot rather than subdued. The entire operation depends upon surprise.

It is important that the residual guard force be constantly on the alert. Specific structural items inside and around the residence are invaluable in buying the needed time for aid to arrive. The windows of the residence should be barred, and heavy doors equipped with quality primary and secondary locking devices should be installed. These would not withstand a long, determined attack but would give the executive and his family time to enter a safe-room.

While this feature might seem somewhat extreme to some, it is not. A safe-room does not have to be a vault; in appearance it is just another room, comfortable and in daily use. It could be the master bedroom or a den.

The safe-room should have but one doorway, quickly accessible to all members of the family. There should be at least one window, guarded with a metal gate locked from inside, allowing for possible escape. Walls must be solid, not of the partition type, and the door should be thick, high-quality hardwood set securely into a sturdy frame. The hinges should be mounted inside the room and secured with long, strong screws. This door should be equipped with a high-quality pin-tumbler lock that operates a heavy deadbolt; there also should be installed a chain or barrel bolt.

The safe-room should be large enough to allow the occupants to stand out of a line of fire from the door. Inside the room, there should be a secondary means of communication and a self-contained loud alarm (Moolman, 1970).

Remember that time is critical to the terrorist; if he can be delayed long enough he will be forced to abandon the attempt and flee to insure his own safe escape. It only requires a delay of ten to fifteen minutes to rebuss most attacks.

Occupation takes the same basic form as the attack, but the aim of the terrorist is to gain entry, seize hostages, and hold them for the following negotiation period. If the safe-room is properly constructed and withstands assault until assistance can arrive, it would be possible for the executive and his family to escape through the windows.

In the event of an ambush, the grounds of the residence would be entered surreptitiously for the purpose of assassination. Adequate security landscaping can make this event unlikely. There should be no high shrubs or thickets, and the grounds should be well lighted with no dark corners nor crevices. The residence itself should be framed in light (Griffin, 1975). Light alone is a strong psychological deterrent. Consideration of the use of patrol dogs is advisable, and patrol of the grounds should never follow a set sequence of time or route.

Execution, kidnapping, sabotage, and bombing all require either penetration or close proximity. In the case of bombing, the bomb must be placed. To accomplish this, the terrorist often relies upon procedural weaknesses in the security system, for example, lack of package inspection, poor tradesman screening, and so on.

The last action mentioned, the war of nerves, is directed against the occupants of the residence and would take the form of obscene calls, telephoned threats, vandalism, interfering with visitors, and other such disturbances. All of these actions are intended to keep the residents in a constant state of discomfort or fear.

It is important to remember that the terrorist requires information. Servants and tradesmen should be questioned frequently to determine if they have been approached for information concerning the house or its residents. The technical security section should periodically conduct unannounced technical surveys of the residence to determine the existence of eavesdropping devices.

To be required to live and function while under constant threat and surveillance can generate great stress upon the residents of the household. This stress is counterproductive to security efforts and can result in the declining efficiency of the executive and the deterioration of the harmonious relationships of the family members.

The security force should attempt to be as unobstrusive as possible and maintain a reasonable distance from family members at all times in order to enhance their feelings of freedom and privacy. In designing the residential security system, one should keep in mind that there is no law stating that security and aesthetic considerations are automatically incompatible. The residence should not be turned into a prisonlike structure.

— Transitory Environment

The executive enters this environment each time he departs his residence or professional setting. The transitory environment represents the most favored period for terrorist activity. There are several reasons for this preference: (1) the time and place of action are the choice of the terrorist; (2) the executive is normally traveling via automobile, the size of this convenience automatically limiting the number of persons surrounding him and thereby assuring the terrorist that he will have numerical superiority; and (3) a vehicle is easily followed, and simulated attacks can be accomplished without the knowledge of the victim.

Jackson (1974) stated that it was later learned there had been "dry runs" on his vehicle. During these simulated attacks, his vehicle was cut off, traffic was blocked, and he was "shot" on several occasions. All of this was, at the time of occurrence, attributed to traffic congestion and the poor driving habits of others. The vehicle is most vulnerable to eight of Marighella's methods of action: attack, entry or break-in, ambush, execution, sabotage, bombing, kidnapping, and the war of nerves.

Other common transitory environments include commercial air travel and hotel lodgings. Within the United States, ground security measures have made commercial air a most desirable mode of transportation. It is one of the most secure modes of travel in the nation with the threat of kidnapping less of a risk factor than in any other means of travel (Private Security Advisory Council, 1976).

In spite of this relative safety, travel plans must still be considered as restricted information. Whenever possible, security personnel should travel in advance of the executive for purposes of securing lodgings and automobiles, becoming familiar with the local area, and learning routes of travel between the lodgings and places of business. It need not be announced where the executive is staying until he actually arrives.

The major threat remains that period of automobile travel between the residence and the office. The first method of action, the attack, would likely take the form of a surprise assault on the vehicle while in transit. When entry or break-in is used, it would be in support of some other method of action, for example, kidnapping or war of nerves. The entry would be surreptitious in nature and might be done to facilitate the installation of a bomb, to sabotage the vehicle to render it an easier target later on, or to plant fake bombs or threats as part of the war of nerves. For this reason, the executive's automobile should never be unattended. It should also be equipped with locks on the hood and trunk as well as on the gas tank.

The tactic of ambush would also be in support of another method of action, perhaps an attack or execution. Marighella urged the ambusher to use light weapons and to kill without hesitation (1971, p. 18):

> Everything depends upon his (terrorist) marksmanship . . . unless he shoots first, he may be killed. And,

> since he will . . . be part of a small group, he must waste
> no time, but shoot quickly.

If conditions warrant, and if the executive utilizes his automobile frequently, it would be advantageous to modify the vehicle. Among these modifications, one should include the placement of steel plate or ceramics inside the doors and behind the seats, as well as the installation of bullet-resistant glass or glass substitute to replace standard windows. Installation of quartz iodine spot lamps and discreet, oversized rearview mirrors also enhances the security of the vehicle. Carefully designed security procedures should be implemented, including the training of the drivers by a reputable school of defensive driving.

Communications play a key role in this particular environment. The central security office should be alerted when the executive begins moving and should receive updated information concerning his location along the route. Central security should maintain specified, coded routes of travel for each executive receiving protection and should communicate the chosen route only minutes prior to departure. These routes should be varied each day to avoid the development of any pattern of travel.

There exists a unique problem common to many individuals in executive positions, that of protocol. Protocol is a hidden enemy of any protective service operation, creating problems by establishing fixed procedures for reasons of etiquette and by forcing undesirable exposure of the executive. Consider the threats posed by protocol requirements in the following situations:

Action	*Protocol*
1. Passage through a doorway ..	Executive preceeds all others
2. Entry into an elevator	Executive enters last
3. Exit from an elevator	Executive exits first
4. Entry into an automobile	Executive enters last

    5. Seating in an automobile ....   Executive occupies
                                             the right rear seat
    6. Exit from an automobile.....   Executive exits first

At formal occasions, security should inquire into the protocol to be expected and should exercise authority over variations to these expectations.

Professional Environment

The last of the three environments, that of the professional setting, should, in theory, be the most secure of all. Despite this increased security, the professional environment is still subject to attack. The office represents the most graphic symbol of commercial interest so propaganda values resulting from an attack on this environment are higher. This environment is subject to all but one of Marighella's methods of action, only the liberation of prisoners is excepted.

During the design of this environment, it is critical that each method of action be carefully analyzed and related to the probable methods of implementation. Planning should include the following areas of concern (Private Security Advisory Council, 1976):

1. Office accessibility
2. Alarm protection
3. Visitor control
4. Key control
5. Safe-room(s)
6. Incoming mail inspection
7. Travel plans

Those offices most likely to be subject to terrorist attempts should not be located on a ground floor and should not be directly accessible to the public. It would be wise to keep stairwells locked and thereby require that entry to the executive office area be accomplished by elevator. Closed circuit television cameras installed in this elevator would allow visual scrutiny of visitors prior to their arrival.

Inside the executive office, concealed alarm buttons should be placed in convenient locations to allow him to summon assistance should the need arise. Alarm systems are important in both the residential and professional environments; great care should be exercised in their selection. One general purpose alarm system would hardly prove adequate for all sections of the home and office structures, so several types should be considered. Alarm systems are simply a means of communicating a warning of potential danger and are normally referred to by the particular principle upon which they operate, that is, electromagnetic, ultrasonic, audio, vibration, capacitance, or photoelectric.

In selecting alarm systems, the following characteristics should be demanded (General Services Administration, 1970):

1. A detection unit or components located at the protected area and designed to initiate an alarm upon intrusion into the area or upon approach to a protected object
2. Signal transmission lines to conduct the alarm signals from the protected area to a continuously monitored panelboard
3. A central annunciating panel containing the components that announce by both visual and audible signals intrusion into and location of protected areas
4. Fail-safe features that give a signal to the central control location when abnormal operating conditions preclude the alarm from operating properly
5. Features that make it less vulnerable to individuals trained to circumvent intrusion detection systems, these features should include capability of concealment and difficulty of neutralization

It is equally important that, after installation, alarm systems be carefully maintained to preclude high false alarm rates. It has been estimated that of all alarms sounded, between 90 and 98 percent are false (Private Security Advisory Council, 1976). Alarm systems should have adequate back-up power service. Electrical utilities in New York and New England have announced an anticipated program of intentional power blackouts in various communities.

Additional controls within the professional environment should include a system of key controls, particularly in critical areas. In the executive area it would be wise to incorporate locking devices that are especially difficult to defeat. One of these is the Medico® lock; the construction of this particular lock renders it all but impossible to bypass or manipulate. Duplication of the Medico key can only be accomplished by certain machines that are registered to bonded locksmiths (Griffin, 1975).

Mastering the locking system throughout the rest of the plant is advisable; this will allow security personnel to gain quick entry into any office or area without first attempting each of perhaps several dozen keys. With a mastered system, one master key will open all those locks within that area of the system but will not allow opening by individual keys. An example of a master lock system is included as Figure 6.

Other areas of security awareness include the procedures established for handling suspicious mail and for maintenance of confidentiality concerning executive travel plans. These and many other areas must be studied as demanded by the particular circumstances of the corporation.

Following the implementation of a security system, the security manager must insure that a continuous program of evaluation is implemented. Security personnel, as well as other corporate employees, should be involved in

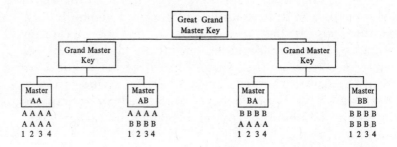

The Great Grand Master Key will open every lock within the system, AA1 through BB4. The Grand Master Keys will open only those locks within their system, AA1 through AB4 or AB1 through BB4. Master Keys will open only the four locks within their systems. Each separate lock, AA1 through BB4, can be operated by its separate key, which will open no other lock.

Figure 6. Master Key System

training sessions frequently to insure that they understand and are capable of maintaining the integrity of the overall system.

CHAPTER 7

Training and Evaluation

Indoctrination and Training

WHEN the subject of private security is raised, many people envision a group of old men, retired and seeking to supplement their Social Security, sitting half asleep inside some warehouse. One assumes them to be a gathering of uneducated, often alcoholic individuals who are unable to hold a responsible job or are too lazy to seek better employment. In the past these evaluations have been all too often accurate.

The National Advisory Committee, in its Report on Private Security (1976), pointed out what it termed the "vicious circle" of private security leading to ineffective performance (Fig. 7). To counteract this vicious circle, it is imperative that the corporation seek to employ qualified people and to insure their retention through a system of adequate salaries, promotional opportunities, and comprehensive training programs.

In addition to establishing training programs for security personnel, it is important that other corporate personnel are exposed to necessary security training. There should exist general security procedures for all employees, including, but not limited to, the following precautions:

1. Avoid giving unnecessary personal details to information collectors in response to inquiries on behalf of publications such as business directories, social registers, or community directories.
2. Be alert to strangers who are on business property for no apparent reason.

Figure 7. The Vicious Circle Affecting Private Security

3. Do not accept delivery of packages from unknown persons or firms unless they have been cleared by the technical services section of security.
4. Use telephones with caution. Do not discuss anything over a telephone that you would not wish an outsider to know.
5. Corporate press releases announcing promotions and so on should not list personal information nor discuss upcoming travel plans or other activities that could be beneficial to terrorist groups.
6. Inform security of any out-of-the-ordinary questions asked concerning a particular executive or security

procedures.

Perhaps the most extensive training, with the exception of the specialized training required of technical services personnel, should be given to those assigned to the transitory and residential environments. These individuals must be able to advise their particular executive concerning areas of security as well as provide him with physical protection.

The drivers of the executive automobile should receive specific training in defensive driving techniques that should include identification and recognition of surveillance, evasive tactics, selection of routes, and communications skills.

The executives themselves should be trained concerning their responsibilities for security and what to expect in the event that they are kidnapped. They must be made to realize that their personal actions while captive determine to a great extent the chances of their safe return. They should be knowledgeable concerning probable treatment by kidnappers. Hacker (1976) divides terrorists into groups according to their main motivations: the crazy, the criminal, and the crusader. This latter grouping is by far the most typical variety. Hacker points out that the crazy most often operates alone, the criminal is organized in a businesslike manner, and the crusader is organized along military lines.

The kidnap victim can expect to be subjected to a tactic favored by the crusader group and by some of the crazies, the tactic of coerced dehumanization. This practice represents a novel perversion in the repertory of human aggression against its own kind, man's inhumanity to man, if you will.

New technological and psychological sophistication has raised the ambitions and possibilities of modern kidnappers. From kidnapping for extortion and blackmail, they have advanced to kidnapping for redistribution of wealth and change of social conditions, and finally to kidnapping for educational purposes. The ideological indoctrination is allegedly performed for the benefit of the victim, who is forced to convert "freely," to demonstrate not just consent but conviction. Coercion, having obscured its brutal origins, is then at its most triumphant when the victim is compelled to experience submission as a voluntary decision. Hacker (1976) referred to this procedure as "rape of the mind."

Crude torture may still break the spirit and the body, but modern thought manipulation, called thought reform or reeducation, succeeds in systematically implanting new and durable inner convictions. The end result is that the victim acts and thinks as he is coerced to do but thinks he does so voluntarily.

In totalitarian countries, the forcibly subjugated citizens are treated as hostages and become victims of coercive tactics. Kidnapping quickly establishes a miniature "perfect" totalitarian society.

The kidnap victim can expect his abductors to employ techniques of mind changing, which often include the following (Hacker, 1976):

1. Sensory deprivation: Incessant exposure to intensive pounding and/or complete isolation. This is highly effective in breaking a person and making him more susceptible to other influences. Human beings cannot tolerate the prolonged absence of sensory stimuli without experiencing extreme frustration and utter confusion, culminating in psychotic episodes. Variety is not the spice but the essence of life. The imposition of sensory deprivation is perhaps the most exquisite form of psychoterror and mind torture.

2. Brain impressing: Terror, i.e., maximum fear produced by intimidation, is a high-tension drive state

that increases the need to respond. The disruption and loss of former structure creates a need for new structure, the destruction of personal identity, i.e., brainwashing, results in alienation, anomie, depression, and withdrawal until, and unless, new ties are formed. Kidnappers are often anxious to show their victims genuine affection and, as often as not, the victims eagerly accept their new friends for the simple reason that they are there.

3. Back in the family: New converts tend to see any absolute authority as increasingly benevolent, understanding, and sincerely interested in their welfare. Total change is more comfortable and hence more frequent than gradual reconciliation of believed differences in resolving cognitive dissonance between traditionally held old and imperatively demanded new attitudes. If submission is inevitable, one might just as well get it over with quickly. The strongest inducement for submission is the lure of a return to a genuine family situation. The new community from which the terror emanates is also, like the family, an agency of love.

4. Monopoly of interpretations: More important than total control over information received by the victim is the exclusive monopoly over all permissible interpretations of that information. The captive gets his news carefully selected and prepared for his digestion. His former community is blamed for everything evil in the world, for the suffering of the terrorists, and the present suffering of the victim. The victim is blamed, but only to the extent that he is still a part of the other, the enemy. The victim is pressured to confess his guilt, engage in self-critique, and turn against all former associates; in so doing he will discover his "real" self.

5. Group belonging: The peer group is the final most important agent of change. Belonging to that group is both the proof and the goal of that change. Since action speaks louder than words, the new convert is required to prove his worth by accomplishing some specific act. If he can be induced to perform some irreversible act with and for his new "family," he is firmly welded to the group by his own internal demands for consistency. He feels compelled to talk and think as he acted. He is now a "new" person, united with the group. The rape of the mind has been consummated.

Equally important as knowing what to expect from a potential kidnapper, the executive must also be educated about his behavior while captive. During this period, the executive should follow these suggestions:

1. Attempt to stay calm. The greatest enemy is despair and fear; maintain self-control and chances of eventual release are enhanced.
2. Do not fight back or struggle. Remember that psychological resistance is preferable to physical resistance. Even if subjected to humiliations and harassment, it is important that the captive not fight back.
3. Comply with instructions by your abductor; do not discuss what actions may be taken by your corporation.
4. Do not provoke the abductor; stay calm and quiet if possible. Be an observer of everything.
5. If code words have been issued by security, use them only if certain that they are recalled in the correct order.

While these steps alone will not guarantee the safe return of the executive, the eventual return will assuredly be jeopardized if they are ignored.

In establishing a training program, it is imperative that one remembers that training never stops. It must be an ongoing and dynamic function. Section supervisors should constantly evaluate the functions within their areas; these evaluations should serve to alert the supervisor in aspects requiring additional attention.

Evaluation and Security Surveys

When the design of a security system is completed and the system has been implemented, the work is still far from finished. The security program must constantly seek to improve itself; to remain the same is to invite disaster. The security manager must assume that his operation is under constant surveillance by others who are as knowledgeable as himself. He cannot afford to relax and become complacent but must implement methods of measurement of program efficiency and effectiveness to insure a consistently high quality of protection. This is accomplished through utilization of security surveys and evaluation.

The security survey is a form of measurement, the application of objective standards to determine potential vulnerabilities and whether or not existing security goals are being met. The results of a survey are then analyzed and evaluated to determine how they can best be utilized to correct deficiencies or to improve existing conditions.

Since security surveys are designed to reflect corporate policy and practices, no single design will fit all corporate programs. The survey should, in general, measure and evaluate the following (Kingsbury, 1973):

1. What and how much security presently exists?
2. Where do the physical and procedural controls exist within the system and how well they are functioning?
3. What are the major vulnerabilities and security threats?

Security survey checklists should be designed to measure

the following areas of the executive protection system:

1. Security policy and management
2. Overall environment threat
3. Professional environment
   a. Building and grounds
   b. Personnel
   c. Hardware
4. Residential environment
   a. Building and grounds (apartment)
   b. Building and grounds (home)
   c. Domestic personnel and operations
   d. Hardware
5. Transitory environment
   a. Vehicle modifications
   b. Vehicle-related personnel
   c. Travel management
6. Crisis plan
   a. Required equipment
   b. Executive biographical data
   c. Crisis team operations

Another unique system of evaluation of the security system is that employed by the Israeli military, known as the "shadow team." In reality, this team is an undercover operation whose members are not known to the security personnel involved in primary security operations.

The shadow team poses as street vendors, taxi drivers, repairmen, and other accepted transients of the particular environment. They observe the primary security force and report any detectable weaknesses or emerging patterns.

The shadow team also serves a second equally important function. They act as a countersurveillance unit, attempting to identify anyone whose activities arouse suspicion. If such individuals were noted, they would be reported to I & I and an attempt to determine their activities and affiliations would be made.

CONCLUSION

TERRORISM, antisocial actions including kidnapping, bombing, and assassination directed against both public and private individuals, is not a relic of the sixties. The threat has not abated. It continues to spread like a communicable disease throughout the world community.

The intent of this guide was to provide the security manager with a didactic source for embarking upon the design of an executive protection system. The writer has endeavored to advance this material in a logical, sequential order conducive to the meticulous planning demanded by such a system.

The reader should realize the magnitude of the task awaiting him if it is his intent to build into his organization a protective system. The writer feels that if the reader has some degree of expertise in the field of security, this book will serve to keep his efforts on track and will assist him in avoiding errors or weaknesses in the final product brought about through omission of consideration of important areas within the system.

BIBLIOGRAPHY

Abrahamsen, David. *The Psychology of Crime.* New York, Columbia University Press, 1967.

Adelson, Alan. *SDS: A Profile.* New York, Charles Scribner's Sons, 1972.

Alexander, Yonah. *International Terrorism.* New York, Praeger Publishers, 1976.

Arrow, Kenneth. *Essays In The Theory of Risk Bearing.* Chicago, Markham Publishing, 1971.

Berger, Lisa. The Insurance No One Will Talk About. *Parade Magazine,* April, 1978.

Bigelow, Robert. *The Dawn Warriors.* Boston, Little Brown & Co., 1969.

Blackstock, Paul William. *Agents of Deceit.* Chicago, Quadrangle Books, 1966.

Bobbitt, H. Randolph. *Organizational Behavior.* Englewood, New Jersey, Prentice-Hall, 1974.

Cleaver, Eldrige. *Eldrige Cleaver: Post Prison Writings and Speeches,* Robert Scheer, editor. New York, Random House, 1968.

Cleverly, Graham. *Managers and Magic.* London, Longman Group, Ltd., 1971.

Cole, Richard B. *Protection Management and Crime Prevention.* Cincinnati, W. H. Anderson Company, 1974.

Criddle, A. Hawthorne. Evaluation of Risks. In Snider, Wayne H. (Ed.): *Risk Management.* Homewood, Illinois, Richard D. Irwin, Inc., 1964.

Farr, Robert. *The Electronic Criminals.* New York, McGraw-Hill, 1975.

FBI National Bomb Data Center Reports, January through September, 1975. Washington, D.C., 1975.

Fearey, Robert A. Terrorism: Growing and Increasingly Dangerous. *U.S. News & World Report, vol. 79,* September, 1975.

Fearey, Robert A. *International Terrorism.* Department of State Bulletin No. 74. Washington, D.C., U.S. Dept of State, 1976.

Forsyth, Frederick. *The Day of The Jackal.* New York, Viking Press, 1971.

Fromkin, David. The Strategy of Terrorism. *Foreign Affairs, vol. 53, no. 4,* July, 1975.

General Services Administration. *Physical Protection, A GSA Handbook,* PBS P 5930.2A. Washington, D.C., U.S. Government Printing Office, 1970.

Griffin, Al. *Home and Apartment Security.* Chicago, Henry Regnery Company, 1975.

Hacker, Fredrick. *Crusaders, Criminals, Crazies: Terror and Terrorism in Our Times.* New York, W.W. Norton & Co., 1976.

Hammond, J.D. *Essays In The Theory of Risk and Insurance.* Glenview, Illinois, Scott, Foresman & Co., 1968.

Healy, Richard J. *Design For Security.* New York, John Wiley & Sons, 1969.

Hickey, Neil. Terrorism and Television. *T.V. Guide, vol. 24,* August 7, 1976.

Houston, David B. Risk, Insurance, and Sampling. *The Journal of Risk and Insurance, vol. XXXI, no. 4,* 1964.

Jack, Homer A. Hostages, Hijacking and the Security Council. *America, vol. 135,* September, 1976.

Jackson, Geoffrey. *Surviving The Long Night.* New York, Vanguard Press, 1974.

Kingsbury, Arthur A. *Introduction to Security and Crime Prevention Surveys.* Springfield, Charles C Thomas, Publishers, 1973.

Laqueur, Walter. The Futility of Terrorism. *Harper's Magazine, vol. 252,* March, 1976.

Lineberry, William P. *The Struggle Against Terrorism.* New York, H.W. Wilson Co., 1977.

Long, Edward V. *The Intruders.* New York, Praeger Publishers, 1967.

Mallin, Jay. *Terror and Urban Guerrillas.* Miami, Florida, University of Miami Press, 1971.

Manchester, William. *The Death of A President.* New York, Harper & Row, 1967.

Marighella, Carlos. *For The Liberation of Brazil.* London, Harmondsworth: Penguin, 1971.

McGinnies, Don C. *Top Man, Reflections of a Chief Executive.* New York, American Management Association, Inc., 1970.

Momboisse, Raymond M. *Blueprint of Revolution.* Springfield, Charles C Thomas, Publisher, 1970.

Moolman, Val. *Practical Ways To Prevent Burglary and Illegal Entry.* New York, Galahad Books, 1970.

Morison, S.E. *The Growth of The American Republic,* 5th ed. New York, Oxford University Press, 1962.

Morrisey, George. *Management By Objectives and Results.* Reading,

Massachusetts, Addison-Wesley Publishers, 1970.

Mowbray, A.H. and Blanchard, R.H. *Insurance.* New York, McGraw-Hill, 1955.

Mueller, Robert Kirk. *Risk, Survival, and Power: Axioms Managers Live By.* New York, The American Management Association, 1970.

National Advisory Committee on Criminal Justice Standards and Goals. *Report of the Task Force on Private Security.* Washington, D.C., U.S. Government Printing Office, 1976.

Oppenheimer, Martin. *The Urban Guerrilla.* Chicago, Quadrangle Books, 1969.

Powell, William. *The Anarchist Cookbook.* New York, Lyle Stuart, 1971.

Private Security Advisory Council to LEAA. *Prevention of Terroristic Crimes: Security Guidelines for Business, Industry and Other Organizations.* Washington, D.C., U.S. Department of Justice, 1976.

Redlick, Fritz. Towards a Better Theory of Risk. In Hammond, J.D. (Ed.): *Essays In The Theory of Risk and Insurance.* Glenview, Illinois, Scott, Foresman & Company, 1968.

Rim, Y. Personality and Group Decisions Involving Risk. *Psychology Record, vol. XIV, no. 1,* 1964.

Roper, C.A. *Locks & Locksmithing.* Blue Ridge Summit, Pennsylvania, Tab Books, 1976.

Shackle, G.L.S. *Decision, Order, and Time in Human Affairs.* London, Cambridge University Press, 1961.

Shaplen, Robert. *The Lost Revolution.* New York, Harper & Row, 1965.

Slovic, Paul. Assessment of Risk-Taking Behavior. *Psychological Bulletin, vol. 61,* 1964.

Snider, Wayne H. *Risk Management.* Homewood, Illinois, Richard D. Irwin, 1964.

Svensson, Arm and Wendel, Otto. *Techniques of Crime Scene Investigation.* New York, American Elsevier Publishing, 1965.

Tannenbaum, Jefforey A. For World's Alienated, Violence Often Reaps Political Recognition. *Wall Street Journal, vol. 198,* January 1, 1977.

Terrorism, Part 3, Hearings Before the Committee on International Security. House of Representatives, Ninety-Third Congress. Washington, D.C., U.S. Government Printing Office, 1974.

Townsend, Robert. *Up The Organization.* Greenwich, Connecticut, Fawcett Publishers, 1970.

Tulley, Andrew. *White Tie and Dagger.* New York, William Morrow &

Co., 1967.

Walls, H.J. *Forensic Science, An Introduction to Scientific Crime Detection,* 2 ed. New York, Praeger Publishers, 1974.

Whitney, David C. *The American Presidents.* New York, Doubleday & Co., 1969.

Wilensky, Harold L. *Organizational Intelligence.* New York, Basic Books, 1967.

Williams, David. *Not In The Public Interest: The Problems of Security in a Democracy.* London, Hutchinson Books, 1964.

INDEX